To Larry,

Hope you enjoy
the book

Mike Corry

"BAD NEWS"

"BAD NEWS"

THE TURBULENT LIFE OF MARVIN BARNES, PRO BASKETBALL'S ORIGINAL RENEGADE

MIKE CAREY

FOREWORD BY BOB COSTAS

SPORTS
PUBLISHING

Sports Publishing books may be purchased in bulk at special discounts for sales promotion, corporate gifts, fund-raising, or educational purposes. Special editions can also be created to specifications. For details, contact the Special Sales Department, Sports Publishing, 307 West 36th Street, 11th Floor, New York, NY 10018 or sportspubbooks@skyhorsepublishing.com.

Sports Publishing® is a registered trademark of Skyhorse Publishing, Inc.®, a Delaware corporation.

Visit our website at www.sportspubbooks.com.

10 9 8 7 6 5 4 3 2 1

Library of Congress Cataloging-in-Publication Data is available on file.

Cover design by Tom Lau
Cover photographs courtesy of Arthur Hundhausen, remembertheaba.com.

Print ISBN: 978-1-61321-963-8
Ebook ISBN: 978-1-61321-964-5

Printed in the United States of America

TABLE OF CONTENTS

Foreword by Bob Costas

In the fall of 1974, Marvin Barnes and I were rookies together in the ABA—teammates in a sense—with the Spirits of St. Louis. He was a first-team All-American from Providence and the nation's leading rebounder as a senior. From among those who were beginning their pro careers that season, only UCLA's Bill Walton, who joined the Portland Trail Blazers, was more highly regarded.

Marvin carried himself with the ease and self-assurance of a born star, which, his future calamities notwithstanding, he absolutely was.

I was a kid out of Syracuse trying to act as if I knew what I was doing—as if I somehow belonged on the same station where Jack Buck was the voice of the Cardinals, where Harry Caray and Joe Garagiola had once been his broadcasting partners.

Marvin and I were each twenty-two, although I looked like I was fifteen. On the court he would often perform incredible feats, and I would do my best to describe them. Off the court, we somehow hit it off. We were always comfortable with each other. And no matter the often-twisted road he followed as his career progressed, we stayed in touch. There were gaps, but we would always reconnect. To be sure, some of what he did was indefensible, but his combination of magnetism, wit, and sheer likability made you want to give him second chances, and then third, and eventually eighth and ninth. After a while, I lost track.

Through it all, over four decades, I was pretty sure that no member of the media knew Marvin Barnes as a player and a person as well as I did. That is, until Mike Carey came along.

Mike's biography of Marvin Barnes is the product of years of meticulous research and vivid personal experiences. I thought I knew Marvin's story, in all its brief glory and squandered possibility, in all its hilarity and tragedy. Turns out, I didn't know the half of it.

But here are two things I always knew. The life of Marvin Barnes is one of the great untold stories in American sports, with enough twists and turns, enough of what was and what might have been, to inspire a novel. The other thing I know for sure was that, as least for a while, Marvin Barnes was one of the best basketball players I have ever seen.

Julius Erving was the personification of the ABA, its greatest and most celebrated player. And yet there were nights when Marvin Barnes completely outplayed him. Didn't just hold his own against him. Outplayed him.

Marvin and Moses Malone broke into the ABA in the same season. Moses would go on to a Hall of Fame career. He would be the NBA's MVP three times. The ABA's Rookie of the Year for the 1974–75 season? Marvin Barnes.

How good was the quality of play in the ABA, a league at first scorned by the NBA but whose three-point shot, slam dunk contests, and celebration of individual flair would soon enough be embraced by the NBA? Good enough that in the first year after the merger (1976–77), 10 of the 24 players in the NBA All-Star Game and half of the 10 starters in the league finals between the 76ers and the Trail Blazers had played in the ABA. And *all* of them would tell you there were times when Marvin Barnes was as good as or better than any of them.

When the NBA celebrated its 50th anniversary in 1997, the league named its 50 greatest players of all-time. I have no doubt that had Marvin Barnes achieved anything close to his full potential, he would have been among them. But the fact that he was not—and the reasons he was not—is what give this story its resonance and poignancy.

This book captures everything Marvin was. Endearing and infuriating. Self-aggrandizing and self-destructive. Fall-down funny and fatally flawed. A wonder and a waste. My unlikely and unforgettable friend.

Preface

What follows is hardly a cold, detached account of the tumultu-
ous rise and fall of Marvin Barnes. Fact is the onetime basketball
superstar, who died on September 8, 2014, at the age of sixty-two
after battling addiction throughout adulthood, was a friend of
mine for more than thirty-seven years. I was his counselor, his
critic, and for most of the final four years of his life, his landlord
and housemate.

We first became acquainted in 1977 when he was playing for
the Detroit Pistons and I was the night news editor at the *Boston
Herald American*. I had written a lengthy article for the Sunday
sports section about the former Providence College All-American
and his many run-ins with the law, including a felony conviction
for attacking a teammate with a tire iron. Barnes, quite predictably, had refused to be interviewed for the piece. "I don't talk to
reporters no more," he told me in a 20-second phone conversation.
"You're all scumbags."

On the day the piece was published, I received an unexpected call. "This is Marvin. Nice story you wrote," he said. "There were a couple things I disagree with, but all in all, you did right by me. Like to meet you one of these days."

"Tell me, Marvin, why would you want to meet with a scumbag?" I said.

For the next 10 seconds, the only sound I heard was his booming belly laugh. "You got me good with that one," he finally said.

A month later, Barnes phoned again, inviting me to visit him at, of all places, the Rhode Island Adult Correctional Institute, where he had just begun serving a four-month sentence for having violated the terms of probation in his assault case by attempting to carry an unloaded pistol onto a plane at Detroit's Metro Airport.

Strictly to satisfy my increasing curiosity about the man frequently referred to in the media as "Bad News," I agreed to sit down with him at the prison. Frankly, I expected to find myself face-to-face with a common street thug. Instead, I found him to be a modern-day Artful Dodger; nothing more than a mischievous overgrown kid. For the entire 30-minute conversation, he entertained me with uncensored, albeit embellished, tales of his Providence ghetto upbringing and his ascension to basketball prominence.

While Barnes was completing his sentence at ACI, he phoned me collect three or four times a week, usually to talk about sports and his experiences behind bars. Shortly before his parole date, he and his fiancée, Debbe, asked me to be the godfather of their infant daughter, Tiffani, an honor that was unanticipated, especially since I had only known the couple for a short time.

Throughout the decades, Barnes and I stayed in close contact as he got himself into one incredibly messy crisis after another. The self-destructiveness, I would discover, was the essence of Marvin, a perpetually misguided soul who never could secure a firm grip on life.

At his best, he was quick-witted, impish, good-natured, hysterically humorous, kindhearted, and generous to a fault.

At his worst, when he was using drugs, he was selfish, deceitful, callous, arrogant, and manipulative to the nth degree.

Although his dark side is impossible to overlook, I, like the many others who cared about him, prefer to remember Marvin for all the times when he was at his best.

—Mike Carey

One

PARTY ON

Naked, with a holstered .44 caliber Magnum slung over his left shoulder, Marvin Barnes, self-proclaimed "Man of Steel," is running the show. On a game night, the Spirits of St. Louis center/forward would have been finishing off a fastbreak with an emphatic slam or swatting some poor sap's shot attempt into the fourth row. But this is an off day, and the reigning American Basketball Association Rookie of the Year is serving as master of ceremonies at an orgy thrown by the Midwest's most notorious and powerful drug trafficker.

It's 1975, and the twenty-three-year-old ABA All-Star is mingling with the partygoers, cracking risqué jokes, and introducing mob bosses to beautiful women at a non-descript two-bedroom apartment located in the northwest outskirts of St. Louis. All of the thirty guests at the invitation-only sex soiree have checked their clothes and weapons at the door. Mountains of cocaine lay atop two large rectangular silver serving trays on the dining room table. Forty quart bottles of assorted top-shelf liquors and row upon row of evenly rolled joints are lined up on the kitchen counter. As the night rolls on, the sounds of Donna Summer,

Chuck Berry, Ike and Tina Turner, Little Stevie Wonder, and Earth, Wind & Fire blare through three-foot-tall hi-fi speakers.

Barnes, as the muscle, gets to carry. If anyone becomes unruly, it's his job to defuse the situation. Yes, he's an intimidating figure, standing 6-foot-8 with the chiseled build of a world-class sprinter. But the physically imposing black celebrity isn't there because he can knock somebody into next week. He's a sports hero in a sports-crazed town who possesses an easygoing, fun-loving personality that is downright charming, which is why he has been asked to host the affair.

Wild times seem to gravitate to the city's most controversial athlete, who is turning partying into an art form. He can play a game one night, stay up well past dawn snorting coke and smoking weed, and then drop 40 on a beleaguered foe some 12 hours later.

Living the life of a gun-toting, drug-using gangster was a role Barnes was born to play. So was being one of the most gifted basketball players on the planet.

At Providence College, he had been one of the country's most dominating big men. During his three-year varsity career, the Friars earned an NCAA Tournament bid each season, including a trip to the Final Four in 1973. He set school records for most rebounds and blocked shots in a game, season, and career, as well as most points and field goals in a game. Remarkably, all those records still stand today. The Rhode Island native could play all three frontcourt positions, running faster than most guards, making supposed defensive stoppers look inept, outjumping much taller opponents, and blocking shots with uncanny timing. At both ends of the court, he was as smooth as the suede suits he wore. In fact, only three-time College Player of the Year Bill Walton was more highly regarded by pro scouts than Barnes.

While an underclassman, Barnes had twice rejected lucrative offers to sign with the ABA's Denver Rockets. Therefore, the logical assumption was that he would showcase his talents in the more prestigious National Basketball Association after having been chosen second overall by the Philadelphia 76ers in the 1974 draft.

Logic, however, seldom played a role in the All-American's decision-making. After only one brief introductory meeting with the Sixers' management, Barnes shocked the hoops world by agreeing to a seven-year, $2.2 million deal with the ABA's Spirits of St. Louis, formerly the Carolina Cougars. For the first time, the NBA had lost a top-three draft pick to its competitor.

The game's purists scoffed at the ABA, with its red, white, and blue game ball, which, at first glance, looked more like a Toys "R" Us novelty item than a legitimate sporting goods product. What most infuriated NBA general managers and coaches, though, was "that damn other league's" helter-skelter schoolyard style of play and its gimmicky three-point shot. In the ABA, critics said, defense was optional. No need for Xs and Os or chalkboards.

To this day, former ABA coaches bristle at the unceasing volleys of potshots that were fired in their direction.

"Anyone who knows basketball recognizes that our league had a positive influence on the game," says Hubie Brown, the Hall of Fame coach who guided the Kentucky Colonels to an ABA title in 1975. "You can start with the three-point shot, which revolutionized offenses and created drama for the fans. We also relied heavily upon tactics such as full-court presses, half-court traps, and zone defenses that few NBA teams used. Sure, our games were faster paced, but that didn't mean there was less strategy involved."

"The NBA was rinky dink and boring," says Doug Moe, who was an assistant to Larry Brown with the Denver Rockets. "We called their style of play 'sludgeball.'"

It was indisputable that the ABA had an ample number of marquee names to promote its product. Julius Erving of the New York Nets was the sport's most athletic player, and no one approached his level of charisma. Power forward Dan Issel and 7-foot-2 center Artis "A-Train" Gilmore of Kentucky, power forward George McGinnis of the Indiana Pacers, and Virginia Squires swingman George "The Iceman" Gervin were all among pro basketball's best.

But the league lacked a national television contract, which meant each franchise depended almost solely on ticket revenue at home games to meet its payroll and expenses. Unfortunately for the ABA, overall attendance was abysmal, which led to constant rumors of impending doom. In fact, three of its ten teams had contemplated filing for bankruptcy after the 1973–74 season. Meanwhile, the NBA, circling like a ravenous vulture, was impatiently waiting to swoop in and snatch up all the top talent once the widely anticipated collapse of its rival took place.

The signing of Barnes offered the ABA at least a sliver of hope for survival. Here was a dynamic player with an engaging personality who had the potential to go head-to-head against the spectacular "Dr. J," as Erving was familiarly known by basketball fans.

Just twenty-four years old, The Doctor was the league's crown jewel, a 6-foot-6 small forward whose speed, leaping ability, and agility created the illusion that he could float through thin air and change direction while soaring to the basket for a one-handed windmill slam or a double-pump stuff.

And there was much more to Erving's game than just his incredible hang time. In 1974, he had captured the league's scoring title with 27.4 points per game while averaging 10.7 rebounds and 5.2 assists to lead the Nets to a championship, and earned MVP honors for both the regular season and the playoffs.

While no one could match the UMass product's gravity-defying dunks, Barnes was being heralded as the total package, a force at both ends of the court who also excelled in the transition game. Now the ABA could promote a series of "Battles of the Titans," with the brash, fearless rookie challenging the league's self-assured, revered superstar.[1]

"Right from the start of his career, Marvin was special, one of my favorites," says Hall of Fame coach Larry Brown. "Besides having all the skills, he had unbelievable natural instincts. I had always thought Bobby Jones, who, in my opinion, was the greatest defensive forward of the seventies and eighties, could stop anybody, but he couldn't handle Marvin.

"Barnes and Bernard King [who won the NBA scoring title in 1985 and amassed 19,655 points during his career] were the quickest players I've ever seen on the blocks. Plus, Barnes had the added advantage of being two inches taller than King. You just don't find guys 6-foot-8 with Marvin's kind of reflexes and speed. He was unguardable. Even as a rookie, he was one of the top five players in all of pro basketball."

Statistics support Brown's assessment. In Barnes's rookie ABA season, he was among the league leaders in rebounding (fourth), scoring (sixth), and blocked shots (sixth). Sixteen times the cocky center scored 30 or more points; on ten occasions he grabbed 20 or more rebounds.

"The guy was an absolute beast," Hubie Brown remembers. "He came into the league, took on veterans like Gilmore, McGinnis, and Erving, and never once backed down."

Ron Boone, a four-time ABA All-Star guard and a member of the Spirits, was in awe of his teammate's abundant talents. "People think I'm nuts when I tell them Marvin was in the same class as

---

1   Utilizing a similar marketing strategy, the NBA would remake itself in the early eighties with the beginning of the Larry Bird–Magic Johnson rivalry.

LeBron James, Magic Johnson, and Larry Bird. It's true, though, because he could control a game all by himself. I witnessed one play against the Colonels where he blocked a shot, tipped it to himself, threw a perfect outlet, and then sprinted past every single defender on the court to catch a return pass for an uncontested dunk. When Barnes felt he was being challenged, he played like a man possessed."

Steve "Snapper" Jones, another teammate in St. Louis, speaks in superlatives when discussing Barnes's aptitude for the sport. "He was the most polished rookie I've ever seen," the former network TV color commentator says. "Not only could he score 25 a night, but his defensive game was flawless. I watched him shut down all the ABA's top scorers. He was so intimidating that players who were All-League were afraid to go up against him because they didn't want to be embarrassed. When opponents had open shots, you could actually see them sneak a peek to make sure Marvin wasn't close enough to move in for a block. He could pounce in a heartbeat.

"His basketball IQ was off the charts. From the get go, he was one of the best rebounders in either league. As soon as a shot was released, he anticipated where the ball would come off the rim and moved into ideal position to come down with it. For him, rebounding was a science. On the boards, he was Dennis Rodman before there was a Dennis Rodman."

As Jones told Terry Pluto, author of the best-selling *Loose Balls*, which chronicled the ABA's nine-year fight for survival, "Marvin thought he was Superman and, for a while, he was."

Perhaps the highest praise for Barnes's abilities came from Barnes himself. "I played like a mercenary, an assassin. Nobody could stop me from scoring or keep me off boards. Anyone who says different couldn't have seen me play."

From day one in St. Louis, the publicity-seeking athlete set out to create an image of a trend-setting, free-spending man about town. Sporting neatly trimmed muttonchops that curled to the corners of his mouth, he chose an eye-catching wardrobe of wide-brimmed floppy hats, gold chains, platform shoes, fur coats, capes, and brightly colored leather bell-bottoms. Constantly surrounded by gorgeous women, he had VIP status at all the hot nightclubs. The sight of him cruising around town in his glistening silver Rolls Royce, equipped with a red mobile phone that cost $2,700, became almost as recognizable as the Gateway Arch.

Clearly, the ABA's wunderkind craved attention from the media and the public. "Broadway" Joe Namath, who had made good on his guarantee to carry the AFL's New York Jets, an 18-point underdog, to victory over the NFL's Baltimore Colts in Super Bowl III, laid down the nightlife template that Barnes sought to emulate. Heavyweight champ Muhammad Ali's gift for gab was equally influential, with the Spirits' star playfully showing off his shadow boxing skills in front of TV cameras while crowing to reporters that one day he, too, would become "The Greatest" in his sport.

Barnes's lofty ambitions, however, would be obliterated by chronic drug use and an obsession for the gangster lifestyle. By 1979, a mere five years after he had made his pro debut, all his swagger was gone. So too was his game. "I've never seen anyone lose so much talent so fast," recalls Rod Thorn, who coached Barnes in St. Louis. "Just a complete waste."

More than a quarter-century has passed since pro basketball's original renegade retired from the sport. A descent into cocaine abuse, involvement in drug trafficking, four and a half years of prison time, and a humiliating struggle to survive homelessness and life on the streets kept his name in the headlines for all the wrong reasons.

In all, Barnes sought to become clean and sober by entering rehab twenty-two times; twenty-two times he failed to achieve success.

Two

THE RUNT FROM APARTMENT 3D

When Al and Lula Barnes, a young couple from the South, along with their two infants, Alfreda and Marvin, moved to Codding Court in the West End of Providence in December of 1952, they thought they had caught a lucky break because rent for their modern one-bedroom apartment in the recently opened subsidized housing project was only $34 a month.

Al, a twenty-four-year-old Navy enlistee, was a six-foot dark-skinned Creole from New Orleans who preferred to bark out orders rather than take them. Lula, two years younger than her husband, was his opposite: shy, sweet, and submissive. A backwoods girl from tiny Lake City, South Carolina, she had just embarked on a career in nursing when she met and married Al soon after he had signed up to serve his country. With a combined annual income of less than $5,500, they scrimped to make ends meet on a nickel-and-dime budget.

The West End had once been a thriving business district anchored by the Gorham Manufacturing Company, one of the nation's leading producers of fine silverware. But when Gorham downsized following World War II, a chain reaction followed that leveled the local economy. The A&P supermarket relocated, an

Esso gas station shut down its pumps, and more than a dozen mom-and-pop stores went out of business practically overnight. Unemployment spiked and the middle class, seeking a fresh start, fled to other parts of the metropolitan area. The remaining residents, mostly African Americans living below the poverty line, felt frustrated, powerless, and isolated.

Still, tenants of the ten-building, 120-unit Codding Court complex on Dodge Street considered it to be a comfortable and safe community setting rather than merely a collection of drab red brick structures linked together in neatly spaced zigzags. Parents looked on protectively as their children played games of "ringolevio" and "tag" on the sparse patches of grass that grew between dwellings. In a corner of the 3.7-acre site was a basketball court. The backboards were undersized, and the nets that hung from rusted, bent rims were, more often than not, in shreds. Sometimes there were no nets at all.

The Barnes household was neither comfortable nor safe. Physical and verbal abuse behind closed doors was an everyday occurrence because Al, a notorious drunk and womanizer, took pleasure in battering his wife. As preschoolers, the children witnessed him repeatedly punch their mother and violently twist her arm simply because she had forgotten to buy green beans for the family's Thanksgiving dinner. "I've never forgotten the terrified look on her face as she begged for mercy," Marvin said decades later.

The innocent siblings were also frequent targets of their father's unprovoked outbursts. Ferocious beatings, inexhaustible threats, and spiteful name calling forced them to live in constant fear. Alfreda, a year older than her brother, vowed to protect him until he was big enough to defend himself against Al's barbaric assaults. Despite enduring countless close-fisted attacks, she never broke her promise.

"This sounds cold," Marvin once said, "but my old man was, by far, the meanest, most evil person I've ever known."

So vindictive and volatile was Al that even when Marvin went to sleep, his head buried beneath the covers, he could not escape an overpowering sense of anxiety. The fragile little boy experienced such vivid nightmares that he'd wake up screaming, drenched in sweat, and trembling uncontrollably. At the tender age of four, he became a bed wetter because he was so petrified of his deranged father, a real-life boogeyman.

Eventually, day-to-day existence became so unbearable that the overwhelmed child often fantasized about killing his tormentor with a butcher's knife. "No lie. I convinced myself that if I could find the courage to do him in, then my mother, my sister, and me could finally have some peace. The man was that much of a monster."

To make sure the peace was kept, there were three unwritten rules that the adult male population of Codding Court considered sacred:

1) Don't snitch;
2) Don't steal;
3) Don't mess around with someone else's woman.

"My father," Marvin said, "definitely didn't give a royal shit about Rule Number 3."

From the manner in which the pompous seaman first class carried himself while strutting through the project's courtyard, it was apparent he fancied himself quite the stud. When he would pay a visit to one of his numerous paramours, he'd often bring his son along to serve as a lookout. While Al was in a neighbor's apartment having sex with somebody else's wife or girlfriend, Marvin dutifully stood guard on the front steps of the building. If the youngster spotted a man walking in his direction, he would race inside, pound his fists on the woman's door, and yell, "Hey, get out! Get out now!" In less than 30 seconds, Al—sometimes not having enough time to put his pants back on—would escape by climbing down a fire escape or jumping out an open window.

The men of Codding Court kept their distance from their surly neighbor, who routinely carried a sidearm for all to see. In their view, he was conceited and, at times, openly hostile. When a few of them finally got together and figured out who was taking advantage of their women, they plotted their revenge. Getting wind of rumors that he was about to become a casualty of vigilante justice, Al, who was about to be honorably discharged from the Navy, temporarily abandoned his family and fled, moving into a studio flat in South Providence.

A mama's boy, Marvin usually spent his free time cooped up at home, playing Monopoly and Risk with his best friend, David Petty, or baking chocolate layer cakes with his sister. When the "runt from [Apartment] 3D," as some of the other kids called him, dared to venture outdoors, he became prime prey for every neighborhood hooligan. In fact, the defenseless weakling would have likely gotten his butt kicked on a daily basis if it weren't for Alfreda, a pigtailed tomboy with a mean streak. She knew all the dirty street-fighting tricks—biting, kicking, punching below the belt, and eye gouging—and wasn't the slightest bit reluctant to use them whenever her brother came under attack.

Shunned by nearly all the children in the projects, the siblings often holed up in their living room, watching gangster movies and *The Untouchables* series on the family's 14-inch black-and-white

DuMont television. Infamous outlaws from the twenties and thirties such as Scarface Al Capone, Baby Face Nelson, Bonnie and Clyde, Lucky Luciano, Bugs Moran, Ma Barker, and Dutch Schultz became their heroes.

"I was going to live fast and die young," Marvin said years later. "I pictured myself at twenty-one, standing alone in the middle of a deserted street, spraying my machine gun into the air as a hundred lawmen came out of nowhere to take me out in a hail of bullets."

A timid personality, however, stood in the way of him becoming an intimidating figure, someone his peers would both respect and fear. His grade-school experiences did little to improve a poor self-image.

He and Alfreda, along with twenty other African American children who lived at Codding Court, walked three-eighths of a mile each weekday to attend Kenyon Street Elementary on Federal Hill, the Italian section of the city. Because the vast majority of the students were Caucasian, the boys and girls from the West End were treated as pariahs.

"Almost all the white kids and even some of the teachers were openly racist," Barnes said. "Once a week, maybe more, I'd get cornered in the schoolyard and had to fight the biggest and toughest bullies. Got the crap kicked out of me every time. During recess, the Italian kids circled around us, screaming out a bunch of slurs. It was their idea of fun." As he said to *Providence Journal* columnist Bill Reynolds, "I was called 'nigger' so often that I forgot my real name was Marvin."

When classes were dismissed for the day, the "intruders" from the projects would run in packs toward their homes to avoid being picked off one at a time by their persecutors, who gathered on street corners, waiting in ambush.

Although Lula was fully aware that her children would be subjected to injustices at Kenyon, she was certain they'd receive a quality education up on Federal Hill. "Schools with the most whites had the most dedicated and experienced teachers," she explains. "The city politicians made sure of that."

At age nine, Marvin, who typically wore oversized T-shirts and denim high-water pants with rolled-up three-inch cuffs, was a mere 55 pounds with toothpick legs and a chicken chest. Basketball, he thought, would be a way to prove his toughness. Uncoordinated and possessing a herky-jerky shot, the puny misfit was always the last one picked to play, if he were chosen at all. "I had no friends on either team, so I was the chump who got slapped around, elbowed, and kneed in the nuts. Everyone on the court laughed at me and called me a spastic."

In 1964, the family scraped together enough money to make a down payment on a three-story fixer-upper on Hamilton Street in South Providence, a mile and a half from Codding Court. They lived on the first floor, with Al, who had landed a job with the postal service, renting out the upstairs rooms to help meet the monthly mortgage installments.

Shortly after moving, twelve-year-old Marvin decided he was now capable of competing in the more physically demanding sports. Taking advantage of his exceptional hand speed and quick feet, he gained recognition as a skillful slap boxer. His success against bigger and stronger opponents led him to give basketball one more try.

The cracked asphalt courts at Bucklin Street Park, seven blocks from home, were his proving grounds. At first, the scrawny newcomer to the neighborhood took quite a pummeling, ignoring intentional karate chops to the throat, kidney punches, and forearm shivers as best he could. After he had picked up a few dirty tricks of his own, the tough-guy reputation he had so desperately sought slowly began to take shape. One day he overheard some of the more experienced players talking about him. "Wouldn't mess with that boy," a husky six-foot street baller said. "Don't look like much, but he crazy. Got some screws loose." Barnes interpreted the remarks as compliments because he knew his days of being regarded as a wimp were now in the past.

By the time Marvin entered high school, the beat cops in District Two considered him a punk, a would-be wise guy who, in reality, wasn't very wise at all. There was much truth to everything the patrolmen had to say about the rebellious troublemaker whose goal in life had once been to become the most cold-blooded black gangster in history.

It's not as if the lippy kid with the king-size chip on his shoulder hadn't attempted to land a steady part-time job. He had, many times, but each without success. The indisputable reality was that black teenagers in Providence had little chance of gaining employment in the mid-sixties. The power brokers at city hall, all of whom were white, took care of their own when it came to doling out cushy municipal jobs. Most of the area's private businesses and unions were, in one way or another, under the control of the Raymond Patriarca crime family, New England's largest and most feared mafia organization. If a high school student was Caucasian and had a connection or two, decent-paying work was not difficult to find.

"I looked everywhere, but the positions were always taken, which really meant they were reserved for whites," Barnes said. "I filled out a ton of applications. Always got turned down. When I realized I wasn't going to be the one black kid from the West End to buck the odds, I threw in the towel. 'Let all them white boys have the damn jobs,' I told myself. 'I'll find a better way to make me some good money.'"

So he recruited five neighborhood friends to help him pull off the first holdups of his outlaw career. The youths' mantra: "By Any Means Necessary." The phrase sounded menacing, but, in truth, the raggedy band of thieves bore no resemblance to today's street gangs that are involved in vendettas, vandalism, and drive-by shootings. Barnes's crew was merely a group of restless juveniles whose illegal activities could only be described as disorganized crime.

Before pulling off a heist, the wayward teenagers usually gathered up their courage by smoking cheap weed and polishing off a half-gallon jug of Boone's Farm Apple Wine as they huddled in an empty equipment shack at nearby Roger Williams Park. "I never touched none of that stuff," Barnes said. "When we were going out on a job, I wanted to be clear-headed."

Using a borrowed gun, the budding delinquents, wearing red bandannas to conceal their faces, robbed three convenience stores before the police began regularly staking out all the local 7-Elevens and Cumberland Farms. "Everywhere we went, cops were eyeballing us. It was enough to scare us off."

The gang's most profitable burglary occurred late one Sunday night when they broke into Morris Clothiers in downtown Providence and stole $2,000 worth of apparel. "After we loaded ourselves up with the nicest threads in the store, we ran out the back door, jumped into our getaway car, and took off," Barnes said. "I waited a month and then stopped into Conte's Tailors on Peck Street to get everything altered. When I got my stuff back, I became the best dressed tenth grader in all of Rhode Island. Man, I had custom-fitted sports jackets and pants for every day of the week."

Three

FIGHTING TO EARN RESPECT

For reasons that were more physical than talent-based, Barnes elected not to try out for the basketball team during his first two years at Central High on Fricker Street. "I thought I had enough ability to win a roster spot, but I took a pass because I was ashamed of my body. I had legs like a girl, ribs that stuck out of my skin and, worst of all, no pubic hair. I was sure my teammates would laugh at me every time I had to undress." So the late-maturing youth stuck with playing in two weekend church leagues simply because he could shower in the privacy of his home.

The self-consciousness faded as Marvin entered his junior year. He was now 6-foot-3 and 170 pounds, looking powerful and athletic. More importantly to him, puberty was setting in. Mentally ready to contend for a spot on the varsity, he signed up for tryouts.

Despite his growth spurt, the inexperienced center was the hazing target of every senior. They pounded him from start to finish during scrimmages, leaving him with an assortment of injuries ranging from dislocated fingers and a broken nose to a series of black eyes. Barnes, whom teammates considered nothing more than a lowly no-talent scrub, shook off all the abuse and used it as motivation.

"I needed to find a way to impress Coach [Jimmy] Adams, but I had no confidence in my moves to the basket. Plus, I couldn't shoot a lick. My strength was playing defense. I had a great sense of timing, could jump higher than anyone on the team, and had a natural feel for blocking shots and rebounding. I knew my best chance of getting noticed was to develop skills that none of the other kids thought were important. I was a thinker. As someone once told me, 'One tactician is worth a thousand foot soldiers.' If I could be the best defender on the team, it would buy me some time to catch up offensively with everyone else."

Marvin made the varsity, listed as the 12th and final player on the roster. As much as he believed his accomplishment was based on merit, Lula played a part. She had phoned Adams before tryouts, explaining in a way only an emotional mother could that her boy would undoubtedly end up in serious trouble with the police unless he was given a place on the team. Out of compassion, the coach promised to find room for her son.

Central had never been basketball juggernaut and, based upon the talent on the 1968–69 roster, Adams wasn't expecting his club to achieve anything better that a .500 record. He also wasn't sure what he had in Barnes.

"My first impressions were that we lacked a dominating rebounder, and we weren't much defensively," said Adams. "Marvin was so raw that I thought it would take him at least a year to make any kind of contribution."

Despite the bleak forecast, Adams's team that season would evolve into what is arguably Rhode Island's greatest.

Determined to carve a niche for himself, Marvin, like any ambitious basketball novice, wanted to establish himself as an indispensable contributor to the team. For that reason, he decided to showcase his toughness on the court by becoming . . . a goon. As a result of his rowdy behavior, he was ejected from his first four varsity games. In fact, two of the reserve center's senseless sneak attacks against opponents led to bench-clearing brawls, which prompted Central guard Robert Fisher to tag him with the nickname "Bad News."[1]

"I didn't much like my new handle, but it sure as hell stuck."

Luckily, Central managed to eke out wins in each of those early-season games. Adams, though, fully realized Barnes's antics were becoming toxic. Following the bench player's fourth disqualification, the coach issued an ultimatum. "Son, you're acting like a buffoon. I don't know what you're trying to prove. All I'm sure of is that you are hurting my team, and I can't allow that to happen. Either knock off all the macho bullshit or turn in your uniform. Your choice."

The stern lecture inspired a perceptible improvement in Barnes's attitude. After every practice, he spent an hour and a half alone in the gym, working tirelessly to develop a consistent shooting touch. When the team's record reached 9–0, he was promoted to the starting lineup.

Meanwhile, tensions were reaching a boiling point at home.

After a loud brother-sister spat had erupted late one afternoon, Al announced that Marvin would be receiving "the beating of his life" following supper. As everyone sat down to eat, the family's sadistic tyrant taunted the teenager by bursting into song. Doing a takeoff on Motown recording artist Sam Cooke's hit tune, he crooned, "We're having a party . . . at eight tonight." Once dinner had ended, Al grabbed a Narragansett Lager from the refrigerator, eased himself into his living room easy chair,

---

1   The Central High standout was not the first player to be nicknamed "Bad News." Jim Barnes, who played for the Celtics in 1969–70, was called "Bad News" by Boston coach Red Auerbach because the reserve power forward inflicted so much punishment on opponents.

and frequently glanced at his wristwatch. What he had no way of knowing was that, a few weeks earlier, his son had bought a .22 caliber pistol from an ex-con who played pickup at Bucklin.

At 8 p.m. sharp, the perverse Barnes patriarch slowly arose and began to rub his hands together, an unmistakable signal that he was about to unleash his fury. But before Al could get close enough to dish out the first punch, Marvin pulled up the front of his shirt with both hands, displaying his weapon, which he had shoved into the waistband of his pants.

"There, now you've got your gun, and I've got mine," said the defiant sixteen-year-old, hands at his side and fingers twitching. "Go ahead, try me. Make your move."

Caught off guard by the show of newfound gumption, Al cursed under his breath and shook his head in disgust. In that instant, he realized his boy's ballsy challenge was no bluff.

As the two silently faced off, Lula stepped between them, blubbering and screeching hysterically until father and son slowly backed away from each other. When the confrontation ended, Marvin, still brandishing his weapon, was banished from the house. For the next two weeks he lived with several teammates' families until he was given permission by his mother to come home on Christmas Eve. Once he returned, the beatings ceased. Al's reign of terror had drawn to a close.

Going into the final month of the regular season, Central's record stood at 17–0. By then, Barnes, who had sprouted to 6-foot-5½, was the team's leading rebounder and shot blocker, having stolen much of the media attention from high-scoring junior guard Ricky Santos, who, in the opinion of most experts, was destined to be the next great college player from Rhode Island.

In the Class A state title game, the dream of an undefeated season would be fulfilled. Santos scored 21 points and earned most valuable player honors as Central beat East Providence,

67–63. Barnes dominated inside, connecting on 11-of-15 shots while pulling down 13 rebounds. The MVP snub failed to upset him. "What's there to complain about?" he said to the media. "I went from twelfth man, to starter, to being voted All State in just five months."

Recruitment letters from major colleges began to pour in, and Marvin seemed to relish the nationwide attention. Still, the impetuous risk taker couldn't resist the adrenaline rush of being a brazen bandit. Less than two weeks after the basketball season had ended, he rounded up his partners in crime and set off on a one-hour rampage.

"We robbed three city buses stagecoach-style. Four of us jumped on at a stop, grabbed all the fare money, and hopped right back off. The drivers didn't know what hit 'em."

After accomplishing their objective, the stick-up artists thought they had made a clean escape. Police, however, had no trouble tracking down the culprits. After all, the "brains of the operation" was the star center on the state's top high school basketball team whose picture had appeared in the *Providence Journal*'s sports section twice in recent months. It didn't take a Kojak to zero in on Marvin Jerome Barnes as a chief suspect.

Fifteen minutes after the gang had fled, cops located the teenagers hiding out in the boiler room of an apartment building and surprised them as they were counting their take—a not-so-grand total of $43.

Following the high school students' arrests, it was rumored that during the holdups, the ringleader had been wearing a Central High championship basketball jacket with the words "Barnes" and "All State" embroidered on the front. While Marvin never denied that he had worn the distinctive coat, he claimed he had turned it inside out moments before committing the crimes.

"I'm sure he was telling the truth," former Rhode Island State Police Superintendent Brendan Doherty says. "The kid wasn't slow. Still, all the officers at the local precinct must have gotten a good long laugh when they saw him walking into the station handcuffed and wearing a team jacket with his name stitched on it."

Informed by a neighbor that her son had been taken into custody and charged with robbery, Lula rushed to the police station.

As Marvin was being led out from a holding cell, his mother took justice into her own hands, grabbing him from behind and repeatedly slapping the back of his head until two rather amused patrolmen gently nudged her away. "Have you lost your damn mind?" she screamed at her boy. "Don't you know all the trouble you're in? All your hard work on the basketball court might not mean a thing now. You may have just thrown away your opportunity to get a college scholarship."

Classified as a youthful offender, the schoolboy hoops hero could have been sent to a detention center for six months. Instead, an extremely lenient juvenile court judge sentenced him to three months' unsupervised probation, after which his criminal record would be sealed.

Days after the case had been resolved, Barnes cut ties with the gang upon learning that a twenty-year-old college basketball center named Spencer Haywood had signed a six-year contract worth a reported $1.9 million with the ABA's Denver Rockets.

"Count me the fuck out," Marvin told his buddies. "I don't want to get into no more trouble 'cause now I know for sure that I can make some serious cash playing ball. College scouts are telling me that I've got what it takes to make it all the way to the pros. If some guy who's only a couple years older than me can be raking in a couple million bucks just for putting his name down on a piece of paper, then I can do the same thing. It's the only way I'll ever earn enough to get out of this hellhole."

As the 1969–70 season began, Adams ran his team so hard in practice that league games were a welcome respite from the intense workouts. To no one's surprise, Central ran the table again, finishing with a second straight 24–0 record and earning another state title with a 57–48 triumph over Sacred Heart from Warwick. In the championship game, Barnes earned the MVP award with a 14-point, 19-rebound effort.

Despite his achievements, New England's most sought-after college basketball prospect found himself mired in a best of times, worst of times situation due to a crisis at home. "I was sure Alfreda was going a little psycho. I knew she had been experimenting with drugs off and on for more than a year. She was pissed off at the world, always picking fights. She looked more like thirty than twenty."

The relationship between the siblings reached an all-time low on the night Marvin spotted Alfreda going into a "sip," a ghetto speakeasy where locals drank, danced, gambled, and dealt drugs. He followed her in and became visibly upset when she sat down next to a girl he couldn't stand.

"What are you doing here with that ho?" he shouted at his sister. "She ain't nothing but an ugly-ass skank." Before he could utter another word, Alfreda dug her fingernails into her brother's arms and hollered, "Start any shit with her and you'll have to go through me."

For the first time, his best friend had taken sides against him. Stunned, he turned and walked out of the after-hours hangout.

Four

AN IMPROBABLE FRIENDSHIP

After leading Central to 48 consecutive wins and two state titles, Barnes was recruited by every college powerhouse except for UCLA, the one school he was hoping to attend.

Coming off a 29–1 season, the NCAA champion Bruins had received early commitments from California's top two high school seniors, 7-foot-1 center Bill Walton and 6-foot-6 small forward Keith "Silk" Wilkes. Legendary UCLA coach John Wooden focused almost exclusively on signing local talent, with the most significant exception having been the successful recruitment of 7-foot-2 Lew Alcindor (later Kareem Abdul-Jabbar) from New York City's Power Memorial back in 1965. "If you were an outstanding home-grown high school player, UCLA was your first choice," Walton says. "The only California kid who ever turned down Coach was Paul Westphal, who picked USC over us, which was a horrendous mistake on his part."

Barnes was never contacted by anyone on the UCLA staff. Even if Wooden had shown an interest, the Rhode Island standout's C-minus grade average and poor SAT scores would have precluded admission to the school.

His second choice was the University of Cincinnati, which had gone 21–6 in 1969–70. Bearcats Head Coach Tay Baker was about to lose center Jim Ard, the team's leading scorer and rebounder, to graduation and had been targeting Barnes for eight months. The coveted blue-chipper eventually traveled by plane to see the school, but didn't quite make it to his destination.

"When I headed out there, it was the first time I had ever flown," he said later. "A half-hour after takeoff, thunder started rocking the plane up and down. The turbulence was so bad that the flight had to be diverted to Baltimore. I was so shook up that once we landed, I cancelled my visit and took a Greyhound bus back home."

Having crossed off Cincinnati from his list of desirable schools, Barnes focused his attention on Providence College, which was only five miles from his home. Labeled a "borderline case" by an admissions adviser, he waited a month and a half for a decision on his application. Finally, Head Basketball Coach Dave Gavitt, who a decade later would become the architect of the Big East and its first commissioner, called and said, "You made it in. You're a Friar."

There were, however, preconditions to being officially accepted to the then-all-male Catholic institution. Barnes, along with eleven other African American students who had below-average high school grades, would be required to attend the Martin Luther King Jr. Summer School program on campus. He would have to take and pass four courses before being allowed to enroll as a freshman.

Although he managed to attain satisfactory grades in all his trial classes, the new resident of McVinney Hall, the tallest building on campus, grew concerned that bigotry might be routinely tolerated on college grounds. "I had dozed off on a couch in the library when one of the professors woke me up, pulled me aside, and told me, 'You can't lie around like that in public. People are going to start calling you a lazy nigger.' Coming out of the mouth of a teacher, those words made me wonder if I had picked the wrong damned school."

His spirits were lifted once he began to develop a rather improbable friendship with sophomore point guard Ernie DiGregorio, a 6-foot Italian kid from North Providence whom everyone simply called "Ernie D."

"People in Rhode Island were already calling him the next Bob Cousy," Barnes said, "but I had seen Ernie play a couple times in rec leagues and, to be honest, I wasn't thrilled about the idea of having him as a teammate. First of all, he was white, which wasn't exactly my favorite color. Secondly, he was way too cocky, or at least that's how he acted on the basketball court. I was also worried about whether he would be looking to shoot all the time. He was supposed to be a pure point guard, an assists guy, but he'd averaged 28 points a game playing freshman ball. In my mind, that meant he had to be a ball hog. Somehow it just didn't sit right with me."

After the pair had spent a few weeks getting to know each other, though, Barnes changed his opinion. Basketball formed the common bond, but there was more to their relationship than just sneakers and nets. "We became close practically overnight," DiGregorio says. "The two of us had similar interests and shared the same goal of making it to the NBA. We started hanging around together all the time, on and off campus. In Providence, being best friends with someone of a different race just wasn't done. There was definitely a 'stick with your own kind' type of attitude. Marvin and me, we didn't pay any attention to that color barrier bullshit."

On the basketball court, the duo meshed perfectly. "We both had great instincts and a passion for the game," says DiGregorio. "I'd kid Marvin that my passing was going to turn him into a scoring machine. He'd tell me that his offensive game was going to make me the country's assists leader. We were just busting each other, but, hey, look how things turned out."

Shortly after the fall semester had begun, DiGregorio invited his new friend to his parents' spacious split-level colonial home for the family's customary Sunday afternoon feast. The buffet-style spread—platters of spaghetti and meatballs, lasagna, eggplant, sausages, hot homemade bread, mashed potatoes, and fresh salad, along with several bottles of wine—dazzled the impressionable dinner guest. Margaret, Ernie's doting mother, took an immediate liking to the wisecracking eighteen-year-old who had a knack for turning on the charm. Not surprisingly, it didn't take long before "Mrs. D," as Barnes called her, began treating him as if he were one of her own. Throughout his college days, Marvin would enjoy countless meals at the DiGregorio home; Ernie was always just as welcome in the Barnes residence.

The first time Marvin brought the flashy playmaker for a pickup game at the Bucklin Street courts, DiGregorio was shown no respect. "All my boys were trashing him, running their mouths about how he was way overrated, bragging about how they were going to school the midget white guy with the stubby legs. Me, I'm just letting them run their mouths. 'Yap all you want, but none of you can stop him,' I told them. Next thing they're calling me a dumb-ass Oreo.

"Well, it took Ernie three or four trips up and down the court to silence all them knuckleheads. He was tossing behind-the-back passes, dribbling through guys' legs, faking everyone out of their jocks. After ten minutes, nobody wanted to guard him because he was making them all look like it was the first time they had ever played the game."

Back in 1970, NCAA regulations prohibited freshmen from competing on the varsity level, but the rules did permit first-year players to work out with the upperclassmen. Every day Barnes and DiGregorio arrived early for practice and stayed late, working on ways to capitalize on each other's strengths. By the start of the 1971–72 season, the pair, now officially teammates, had developed some serious chemistry. Ernie D was perhaps the slickest passer and ball handler in the country; Marvin possessed all the physical tools and post-up moves to become one of college basketball's most formidable inside players.

Two weeks before making his varsity debut, Barnes walked into a Chinese restaurant near campus for lunch. As he was about to sit down and place an order, two brawny middle-aged white men dressed in polo shirts and black chinos entered the dining area and invited him to join them at their table. Assuming they were Providence fans, probably alumni, he pulled up a chair.

"Marvin, we're professional gamblers," one of them matter-of-factly mentioned less than 90 seconds into the conversation. "We're always looking for a little edge when we place a bet. You can help us, and we can help you. Let me tell you how. Say you're playing UConn, and a few hours before tipoff one of the other starters comes down with the flu. You hear that the guy is sick as a dog and won't be able to play. All you have to do is make a phone call and clue us in. You'll get $500 for giving us the heads-up. Nobody but you and us will ever know.

"Or let's say you're playing some rag-tag team and you're 20-point favorites. We'd put our money on the underdog. Maybe you miss a few shots and make a bad pass or two. Providence would still win by 15, and we'd take real good care of you for doing us a big favor."

Now surmising that the apparently mafia-connected bettors had tailed him from school to the restaurant, Barnes didn't know how to respond, so he stalled. "Just give me a day to think it over," he said, "and I'll get back to you."

Repeatedly glancing over his right shoulder after leaving the restaurant, "Marvin the Magnificent," as *Sports Illustrated* had referred to him in its preseason college basketball preview, headed straight to Gavitt's office and related every detail of the stressful encounter. "I'll take care of things," the coach coolly told him. "I promise that you've seen the last of those clowns."

The two gangsters never contacted Barnes again.

Brendan Doherty says how the up-and-coming twenty-year-old would have been a logical mark. "Fixers usually make their pitch to the top players, particularly the ones from poor families who could be easily tempted to make some quick cash. These sleazebags have a way of convincing kids that point shaving is foolproof," the former law enforcement official says. "Back in the seventies, sports gambling was a booming industry in Rhode Island because the Patriarca crime family controlled the bookie business. I'd go around to all the local colleges and give talks to players about how they would be in jeopardy of throwing away their futures if they attempted to manipulate the point spread or lose games outright. In Marvin's case, he'd have been putting a pro career at risk if he shaved points even once. For maybe five hundred bucks, he could have cost himself millions. Fortunately, he did the right thing by reporting the incident to his coach."

That was not the last time the sophomore would be approached with a business proposition. After a preseason practice, a local hustler named Bill Bailey pulled him aside and initiated a conversation, speaking in a hush-hush tone. The pushy pitchman wanted to arrange a clandestine private meeting between Barnes and Bob Woolf, a pioneer in the sports representation field. Curious and flattered, the pro prospect agreed to sit down with the well known Boston-based lawyer.

Woolf first began working on behalf of athletes in 1964 after he had won a favorable verdict in an auto accident case for Red

Sox pitcher Earl Wilson, who soon hired him to negotiate his baseball contract. Thanks to a great deal of positive publicity in the media, the attorney's client list steadily grew to include members of all the pro teams in Boston, including such high-profile players as Red Sox sluggers Carl Yastrzemski and Ken "Hawk" Harrelson, Patriots quarterback Jim Plunkett and wide receiver Randy Vataha, Bruins center Derek Sanderson, and Celtics swingman John Havlicek all signing on. Years later, the influential agent would represent his most famous client, Larry Bird, as well as many other NBA All-Stars.

Bailey, who was employed full-time by Woolf, made his living by being a "runner," a recruiter of talented young players. The sweet talker's responsibility was to persuade the cream of New England's college crop that no one could negotiate more lucrative contracts than his boss. "I remember the guy yakking a mile a minute, telling me that I should be honored that a big shot like Bob Woolf was interested in me because he only represented superstars. And I believed every word that came out of his mouth."

A day later, Bailey drove the potential early first-round draft pick to Woolf's two-room office in Brighton, Massachusetts, where large framed autographed color photos of the attorney chumming it up with broadly smiling clients decorated every wall. "Bob was a distinguished-looking guy, soft spoken, and very sincere," Barnes said. "Or so I thought."

During the first few minutes of the get-acquainted meeting, Barnes innocently referred to the athlete representative, who had been a guard on the Boston College varsity basketball team in the late forties, as an "agent."

Woolf interrupted his guest mid-sentence. "Son, I'm a sports attorney, not an agent," he said, sounding deeply offended. "I earned my law degree at BC many years ago. I worked extremely hard for it. Most so-called agents have never seen the inside of a law school or a courtroom. They're a bunch of worthless swindlers who care only about making a fast buck."

"Yes, sir," Marvin replied. "Got it straight now."

The forty-four-year-old contract expert emphasized that his clients—athletes, coaches, actors, and TV newscasters—were all like family to him. "They come down to my summer place on the Cape all the time," he said. "Every weekend is open house. We have great food, great conversation, and plenty of laughs."

After the soft-sell spiel, Woolf got down to the nitty-gritty of the discussion, proposing a tantalizing deal to the cash-strapped underclassman. "Look, I want to represent you when the time comes. We can't sign a formal agreement while you're still playing for Providence, but what I can do is lend you some money. I won't charge you a dime in interest. All you have to do is agree to pay me back once you sign your pro deal. What I'm really asking from you is your loyalty."

Barnes was blown away. "Woolf told me he would give me $200 a week and help out my mother with her bills. If the man came through like he was promising, I'd be on easy street."

The sports bigwig slid two copies of an already filled-out promissory note across the desk, and his prospective client signed them without even reading the document. As Barnes stood up to leave, Woolf handed him eight crisp hundred-dollar bills, the first monthly loan installment. To seal the deal, the two shook hands while Bailey took a few Polaroid snapshots for his boss.

"Even though I knew accepting money from an agent wasn't exactly on the up-and-up, I felt like I had just attended a meeting that was going to change my life. And it did, just not in the way I was expecting."

Five

HANDLING SUCCESS . . .
AND FAILURE

Six days after receiving an unanticipated helping hand from Bob Woolf, Marvin, playing in his second varsity game, grabbed 34 rebounds and blocked 12 shots—both school records that still stand—in a 76–58 romp over Buffalo State at the sold-out Alumni Hall. The masterful individual effort, which also included scoring 18 points, convinced the 3,400 in attendance that they had witnessed the birth of a Friar messiah.

On campus, however, the pride of the Codding Court projects was troubled by the attitude of many supposedly prim and proper white students. Because there were only thirty-eight African Americans enrolled among a student body of 2,550, the ill-at-ease undergrad faced a distinct culture clash. "To put it mildly," he would later say, "blacks weren't exactly welcomed with open arms. In my dorm, we were treated like we had some highly contagious disease."

By the middle of the school year, Barnes felt unwanted and mistrusted. His expressionless demeanor did not go unnoticed by the faculty. One day he was summoned to a meeting with Father Walter Heath, the supervisor of dormitory residents. "Marvin, you don't interact with anyone except your teammates. Is there a problem?" the priest asked. "You never show any emotion. Smile once in a while, will you?"

"There's nothing to smile about," the student-athlete replied defensively. "My life here isn't about cracking jokes and making friends. I'm not trying to win no popularity contests. I'm just working hard to get my degree."

"Look, here's our concern," the spiritual counselor replied. "You always seem angry. The way you look at people, it's scaring them."

Scaring *them*? In the basketball star's view, it was he who felt distressed by the icy stares he received from all the PC preppie types, with their crew cuts, Izod knit shirts, Irish wool sweaters, and tasseled brown penny loafers.

"Father, I just want to get along," Marvin said, attempting to end the strained dialogue. "I don't act like a snob or a big shot, and I'm not looking for any hassles."

The basketball team became Barnes's family on campus. In addition to his friendships with black teammates and Ernie DiGregorio, he grew close to two other white players, forward Fran Costello and Kevin Stacom, a guard from Queens, New York, who had recently transferred from Holy Cross. Being surrounded by fellow athletes whom he totally trusted was now the only way he could be himself, relaxed and lighthearted.

"News was always joking around," Costello remembers. "It seemed like every day there was a new Marvin story floating around the locker room. It might have been about him and one of his girlfriends. It might have involved some off-the-wall stunt he pulled at practice or something he said to Coach. What stood out to me was that he never had a problem poking fun at himself."

Providence entered the 1972 NCAA tournament with a 21–5 record. The Friars, though, had faced only one Top 10–ranked opponent all season (a 70–66 victory over No. 7 USC) and were routed, 76–60, in the opening round by the 2nd-seeded University of Pennsylvania.

Barnes averaged 21.6 points and 15.8 rebounds in his first varsity campaign. DiGregorio also put up impressive numbers, racking up 17.7 points and 7.9 assists per game. The outlook for the 1972–73 season was highly promising, especially with Stacom, a deadly outside shooter, becoming eligible to compete.

It was increasingly evident to Barnes that his celebrity status could lead to receiving special treatment. A few weeks after the tournament, he was walking down Huxley Avenue toward the gym when DiGregorio slowly coasted by in a shiny new dark green Corvette Stingray, complete with a vanity license plate that read "Ernie D."

"Hey, man, where'd you get the wheels?" Barnes shouted.

"I used my room and board money to buy it," DiGregorio, who lived at home while attending school, replied.

"Oh, yeah, well, I need to get me something classy, too," said Barnes, who proceeded to walk to the athletic office, where he inquired about how to obtain a vehicle as sharp as his teammate's.

The following day he and his mother were driven by an alumnus to Tasca Ford, where the basketball star picked out a 1972 four-door yellow LTD, with brown leather interior. "Don't forget, put 'News 24' on the license plate," Marvin told the salesman before leaving the dealership.

"Never did find out who paid for the car," he said years later. "To be honest, I didn't want to know and didn't care. All I can say for sure is that my mother and me didn't have enough money to buy a used bicycle, let alone pay for a brand new luxury automobile."

Once Barnes took possession of the vehicle, there was one major obstacle for him to overcome: He had virtually no driving experience. During the first month behind the wheel of his stylish sedan, he was involved in two fender benders, both of which were his fault. He also backed into a fire hydrant while attempting to parallel park, creating a geyser that sprayed a forceful stream of water 20 feet into the air. "Funniest thing I've even seen," recounts teammate Mark McAndrew. "There was Marvin stranded in his car on a flooded street as thousands of gallons of water poured down onto his car roof like Niagara Falls. It was something straight out of a TV cartoon."

In May of 1972, the sophomore, whom the ABA classified as an underclassman free agent, was offered a two-year $300,000 guaranteed contract by the Denver Rockets. "I knew I could eventually do a lot better by staying put, so I turned down the deal. It was a no-brainer," he said years later. "What you've got to understand was that I wasn't hurting for cash because Woolf was sending me my eight hundred [dollars] every month like clockwork."

Having passed up the chance to play professionally in the Mile High City, Barnes was given an opportunity to shine on a much more prestigious stage when he was chosen to try out for '72 United States Olympic basketball team. A total of 67 players would compete for 12 roster spots, plus two alternate selections, during a two-week training camp at the Air Force Academy in Colorado Springs.

Surprisingly, College Player of the Year Bill Walton was a no-show. The UCLA center, who was recovering from a foot injury and tendonitis in both knees, had been invited but declined. While no official explanation was given, the media reported that Bruins Coach John Wooden had advised his star to rest the entire offseason. There was also speculation that the Academic All-American would have been agreeable to joining the team if he were permitted to skip training camp. According to the rumors, US Head Coach Hank Iba rejected the bold proposal. Another theory was that Walton, an anti-war activist who had been arrested at a recent student demonstration, was boycotting the international competition in protest of US policies in Vietnam.

No matter what the actual reason, his absence didn't appear to be a catastrophic setback because the Americans had never lost a game in Olympic competition (63–0), having won seven gold medals going into the '72 Munich Games.

At tryouts, the candidates were divided into eight teams. Barnes was outstanding during the two-a-day scrimmages, finishing as the leading rebounder and shot blocker, as well as the fifth-leading scorer, in camp. His principal competition at the power forward and center spots were Minnesota's Jim Brewer, Maryland's Tom McMillen, American University's Kermit Washington, North Carolina State's Tom Burleson, Houston's Dwight Jones, Walton's UCLA backup Swen Nater, and North Carolina's Bobby Jones.

"Talent-wise, Marvin was among the top players in camp," says former NBA coach Doug Collins, who was a starting guard on the '72 squad. "Everything he did looked effortless. The game came easy to him."

The final roster, except for one selection by Iba, was chosen by a 52-man committee. "There were coaches and commissioners from every level of the NCAA, the NAIA, junior colleges, the AAU, and even the Armed Forces on that panel," said John Bach, who was an assistant coach for the US team. "It was very political, sort of a 'you vote for my guy and I'll vote for yours' type of thing."

In the end, Barnes didn't make the cut.

"Most of the guys at tryouts had never played against each other," says Collins. "We basically had fourteen days to learn everybody's strengths and weaknesses. We were all young, right around twenty years old. I think the committee's main concern was selecting a team that had the capabilities of becoming a cohesive unit. For some unknown reason, I guess they didn't believe Marvin fit their needs."

Collins wasn't the only player on the team who was puzzled by the decision to jettison Barnes. "If I had to pick one guy to be in the trenches with me when we went into battle, it would have been Marvin," says Ed Ratleff, a 6-foot-6 swingman from Cal State who made the squad. "He wasn't dirty, but he was extremely physical, a guy who was always ready and willing to protect his teammates."

Barnes believed his militant image cost him a spot on the roster. By his own admission, he was someone who could be argumentative and, at times, combative. "I wasn't your basic milk and cookies black guy who was polite, well-spoken, and always on his best behavior. I came straight out of the ghetto. I was a bit of a wise ass, ready to mix it up with anyone. One time I smacked McMillen right across the face after he elbowed me, and that caught the coaches' attention. I guess Iba thought I was loose cannon because he never gave me a reason for why I got cut."

Then–Boston Celtics coach Tommy Heinsohn watched the tryouts for a week. "The decision-makers must not have been paying any attention to the scrimmages because Marvin was, by far, the most impressive player on the court. He got every rebound, and no one could stop him from scoring. How could you leave a guy like that off the team? It made no sense."

By the time the finals rolled around, only the Russians stood between the Americans and the gold medal. The more experienced Soviets, whose average age was twenty-six, had trained together seven days a week for two and a half years, having played more than 90 games as a unit internationally prior to the '72 Olympics. In reality, they were professionals, all being paid generously as full-time officers in the Red Army.

The US opponents played a slowdown style that sucked the air out of the ball. Iba, strictly an old-school strategist, decided his team could beat the Russians at their own game by using a similar plodding offensive attack rather than attempting to capitalize on his youthful players' speed advantage by forcing an up-tempo pace.

"We had the wrong damn coach," Ratleff says. "His first dumb mistake was cutting Marvin. His second came in the finals when he wouldn't let us use our fastbreak to run the Russians right out of the gym. Not one guy on our team agreed with Iba's game plan."

The end of the Olympics gold-medal game between the two undefeated teams has remained shrouded in controversy to this day.

With just one second showing on the clock, the US took its first lead of the contest, 50–49, when Collins, despite having been knocked unconscious after being slammed into the basket stanchion on a fastbreak drive, recovered and put in two free throws. The Americans thought they had the victory in hand. That's where confusion took over.

A fraction of a second before a still-groggy Collins drained his second free throw, a horn from the scorer's table had sounded in error. At the direction of William Jones, the British co-founder of the International Federation of Amateur Basketball, who had no legitimate authority at the Olympics, the referees counted the foul shot but ruled there were actually three seconds remaining in the game.

After the ball had been inbounded, one official blew his whistle as the Soviets struggled to bring the ball past midcourt as time was about to expire. As the Americans began to celebrate their apparent victory, the Russian coaches argued that they had called a timeout before Collins attempted his second free throw. The referees dismissed the claim, but, at the insistence of Jones, decided that the clock would be reset to three seconds and the inbounds pass would be replayed.

The Soviets followed by attempting an 88-foot heave that missed its mark as time ran out. Once more, Team USA rejoiced. The refs, however, declared that as the ball was being put into play, the clock was still in the process of being reset. Therefore, the play was nullified.

On the third "do-over," 6-foot-8 Soviet center Alexander Belov caught a fullcourt pass, collided with 6-foot-7 Jim Forbes, sending him sprawling to the floor, and put in the game-winning layup.

US officials filed a formal protest two hours later, but the rules committee upheld the Russian victory by a 3 to 2 vote, with three communist bloc nations voting against the appeal.

So angry and distraught were the Americans at how the Soviets had been handed the win that they refused to accept their medals and boycotted the awards ceremony. "We weren't going to sell ourselves out for a few pieces of silver," shooting guard Tom Henderson says. Today, those medals, never presented and never worn, are stored in a vault in Lausanne, Switzerland.

Watching the game on TV by himself in his mother's living room, Barnes was seething as the most bizarre three seconds in basketball history played out for an agonizing six minutes in real time. "If Iba had kept me on the team, if I had been on the court for that last inbounds pass, there was no way it would've worked. I was stronger, faster, and could jump higher than all them Commies. Guaranteed, Belov never would have gotten a hand on the ball. I looked at replay after replay, and all I kept saying to myself was, 'What a crying shame.'"

Six

THE TIRE IRON INCIDENT

Before the start of the 1972–73 season, Barnes was summoned to Gavitt's office for a potentially thorny discussion concerning how the coach intended to boost the draft stock of Ernie D, the Friars' senior All-American candidate.

"Marvin, don't take this the wrong way, but this is going to be Ernie's year," Gavitt said. "I'm going to be talking him up every chance I get. We've got to make sure he's a top-five pick in the draft. After he goes pro, then it will be your turn to be in the spotlight. I'll do everything in my power to get you the kind of contract you deserve. You did the smart thing in turning down Denver's [$300,000] offer. Now it's my job to help you make a lot more money than what you could have gotten."

The strategy was wholeheartedly endorsed by Barnes. "Hey, Dave, we've got the best damn point guard in the country. That's just fact. Whatever you've got to do to make people see that, I'm all for it."

Once Gavitt was assured that his plan had been well received, he joked about the dilemma he'd been facing. "It's always difficult to promote one player over another, especially when it's you and Ernie who are involved. I can't win no matter what I do. If I don't rave about you, I'll get stabbed by one of your ghetto friends. If I don't praise Ernie, I'll get shot by one of his Mafioso buddies."

But the laughs stopped on October 19, 1972, when Barnes assaulted teammate Larry Ketvirtis outside the school cafeteria hours after an elbowing incident during a team workout.

A lumbering white reserve center with an ornery disposition, Ketvirtis, who had averaged only 5.9 points and 3.6 rebounds in his first varsity season, carried 220 pounds on his 6-foot-10 frame. He was a bruiser who didn't think twice about injuring someone—and that was just in practice.

Ten days prior to the conflict between the pair, six members of the varsity team had marched into Gavitt's office, demanding that Ketvirtis be dismissed from the team or, at the very least, banned from practices. They were fed up with his excessively aggressive fouling that had resulted in black eyes, sore jaws, broken noses, and other miscellaneous battle wounds. Let the out-of-control hatchet man participate only in games, the players argued, where opponents, not teammates, would be in jeopardy of physical harm.

Gavitt flatly denied their request. "Larry plays a key role on this team. He's our enforcer. He gives us a degree of toughness that we need to be successful."

The one voice conspicuously silent throughout the summit meeting was Barnes's. "I was the only guy who *didn't* want Ketvirtis booted off the team," he said later. "If we lost him, it would mean I would end up playing all my minutes at center rather than power forward, my natural position. I'd still get my points and rebounds, but I'd have to work a lot harder for them because I'd be going up against guys who outweighed me by 20, 30 pounds."

Furthermore, Barnes concurred with his coach that the Friars needed a butcher who possessed enough sheer nastiness to intimidate the opposition. "Larry loved all the contact, legit or not.

I watched guys on other teams quit fighting for position because they couldn't take any more of his pushing, grabbing, kneeing, and hacking. He was as dirty as they come, which was great for us."

On the day that would have a profound effect on both players, the squad's two big men were matched up against each other during an informal four-on-four scrimmage. "I was standing maybe three feet away from Ketvirtis when he came up with a loose ball and, for no reason, threw an elbow," Barnes said. "Nailed me right on the mouth and knocked back two of my lower front teeth. They were so loose that I could have pulled them out with my fingers."

Bleeding profusely from a deep quarter-inch gash inside his lip, he spit out a glob of blood and walked unsteadily into the locker room. Gavitt, who had been watching from the stands, followed behind. "You know, this wouldn't have happened if you hadn't been bullshitting around out there," the coach coldly remarked.

The snide comment infuriated Barnes. "*Bullshitting around? I was just playing basic defense," he yelled back. "How the fuck can you blame me for what happened? What were you looking at, anyhow, Dave? Just add my bashed-in teeth to the list of injuries we bitched about to you the other day."

His mouth swollen and stuffed with wads of cotton to contain the bleeding, Barnes was driven to a dentist, who cemented both teeth back into their sockets. The damaged incisors, however, were so torn from their roots that nothing could be done to save them permanently.

Returning to campus, he stopped by the Raymond Hall cafeteria and spotted Ketvirtis sitting with two freshman players, Mark McAndrew and Rick Dunphy. Instead of confronting his apparently remorseless teammate, Barnes sat down at a table across the room. That's when Tom Walters, a reserve guard, egged him on: "You can't let that bonehead think he can get away with that nonsense. Call him out."

Swallowing the bait, Barnes motioned for Ketvirtis to step outside. The ensuing conversation did not last long.

"Look, Larry, I can take whatever you got," Barnes said, "but there are other guys who think you're dangerous, that you're destroying this team. They want you gone."

"Well that's too bad. It's their problem," Ketvirtis replied. "You really think I care about anything that you've got to say?"

"Man, you just about knocked out two of my teeth," Barnes shouted back. "At least hear me out."

"Hey, that's life, pal," the second stringer replied as he was turning away to walk back into the cafeteria.

Irate, Barnes delivered a blow to the face, knocking his teammate into the building's entrance door. He always maintained he threw a punch. Ketvirtis, on the other hand, eventually claimed he was hit with a tire iron.

Barnes insisted he was not in possession of a weapon when he struck Ketvirtis but did admit that following the heated confrontation, he retrieved a tire iron that he had hidden in a nearby bush. "The two of us came out of Raymond Hall at the same time," Barnes remembered. "Don't you think the guy would have noticed right away if I had been holding a tire iron? I was standing right in front of him, maybe five feet away, and we argued for at least a minute or two. He was looking right at me. If I had something that big in my hand, do you think he would have just stood there?

"After Ketvirtis went inside, I ran over to where I had stashed the tire iron, picked it up, and carried it into the cafeteria with me. I wanted to make sure he saw me holding it so he wouldn't attack me, but I never had any intention of using it. All I wanted to do was keep the guy from charging at me, just like an animal trainer uses a chair and a whip to hold off a lion from mauling him."

As the two stood ten feet apart from each other in the cafeteria, a clearly shaken Ketvirtis, continually pointing at the tire iron in his teammate's right hand to attract the attention of student onlookers, called for a truce. "Look, I don't want to fight," he yelled. "Put that thing down and we'll talk." Barnes slowly took four steps backward before dropping the foot-long black steel rod, which was immediately carried away by a staff worker on the scene.

After a few tense moments, the pair left the building through separate exits. Father Heath assessed Ketvirtis's injuries shortly afterward and would later say, "Larry had a bump on his cheek and a small cut, just like hundreds of battle scars I've seen on kids who had gotten into minor fights over the years."

According to Gavitt, Ketvirtis didn't allege he had been struck by a weapon—at least not on the day of the attack. "When my staff and I met with Larry an hour after the incident," the coach said, "he never mentioned anything about Marvin hitting him with a tire iron—and we talked with him for quite some time. What he told us was that he was hit from behind by a sucker punch."

Following the meeting with the coaches, Ketvirtis was driven to his home in Milton, Massachusetts, by a staff member. Later that night, he was examined at Carney Hospital in Boston, where X-rays showed he had sustained a fractured cheekbone.

"If I had used a tire iron to hit the guy," Barnes said, "don't you think he would have immediately filed charges and gone straight to a hospital near campus? Well, Ketvirtis didn't do either of those things. What I think happened is that once he got home, he talked to some lawyer who told him to see a doctor ASAP. Larry knew damn well I was going to be getting a bundle of money when I turned pro. This was his chance to cash in big time if he played his cards right."

Days after the incident, Providence College officials held a disciplinary hearing. As a result of the inquiry, Barnes was placed on probation but allowed to continue playing basketball.

Ketvirtis, declaring that he had been the victim of a cover-up by the coaching staff and school administrators, withdrew from the school days after the ruling had been issued. "The fact that Marvin Barnes received total immunity was intolerable," he said weeks later. "I just wanted to get away from that place."

On December 13, 1972, nearly two months after the physical conflict, the self-exiled former Friar filed a police report in Providence. A grand jury subsequently indicted Barnes for felony assault with a dangerous weapon.

Before the start of the criminal proceedings, the prosecutor offered a plea deal of a year's suspended sentence and three years' probation. Defense attorney Alton Wiley advised his client to accept the proposal. Woolf, acting as an unofficial consultant, agreed with the recommendation. "There's a great amount of money at stake here," he explained to Barnes. "If by any chance you're found guilty, you'll have to go to prison for a minimum of two years. Not only will your market value go down, but you won't even be able to start your pro career until you're twenty-four or twenty-five."

The guidance was emphatically rejected after Lula tearfully begged her son not to admit guilt for a crime he did not commit. "For the last time, I ain't copping no plea," Marvin told his lawyers. "The only thing I hit that man with was my fist."

A day into the trial, however, the embattled defendant relented and grudgingly accepted the prosecutor's terms. "I told the judge that the only way I'd plead guilty was if I could state for the record that I did not use a tire iron. He agreed to let me say my piece as long as I mentioned that based on the evidence, it was a possibility that the jury could convict me. In my heart, I know I would have been found innocent. It all boiled down to the fact that I couldn't risk serving time because then I'd lose everything I had worked for, including my scholarship and all the money I'd make during my first few years as a pro."

The compromise judgment did not put an end to the matter. It was inevitable that once Barnes signed a pro contract, Ketvirtis would be seeking a seven-figure sum in damages by filing a civil suit.

Seven

MAKING A RUN
FOR THE NCAA TITLE

Out in Vegas, oddsmakers installed UCLA as the prohibitive 4-5 preseason favorite to capture the 1973 NCAA title. Placing a wager on any other team appeared to be the ultimate sucker's bet because the Bruins were coming off a 30–0 season, which had earned them a sixth straight national championship. During the incredible run, John Wooden's elite troops had compiled an overall record of 175–5.

For the upcoming campaign, UCLA would be led by Walton, whose supporting cast included Wilkes, 6-foot-8 power forward David Meyers (the nation's top-rated sophomore), and 6-foot-11 backup center Swen Nater.

Providence was one of only a handful of teams given even a remote chance of taking down the West Coast Goliath. In the open court, Barnes could test the endurance of Walton while DiGregorio was as capable of quarterbacking the break as any point guard in the country. Complementing the up-tempo attack would be the perimeter shooting of Stacom. "Without a doubt, Kevin was the best practice player I've ever seen," said Barnes. "He'd hit ten straight from out deep and then get all mad at himself if the next one rimmed out. In games, though, he was too unselfish. He'd have an open shot and still be looking to pass. We'd all be wondering why he didn't just knock down the jumper. A 20-footer for him was like a free throw for anybody else. He was that good."

Gavitt believed in turning his players loose, with DiGregorio choreographing the run-and-gun offense.

"Gavitt knew how to get the most out of each player on the roster," recalls Stacom, who has now been a pro scout for more than twenty-five years. "He had a knack for mixing and matching. He'd always have five guys on the court who would work well together because he knew everyone's personality. Marvin and Ernie liked to put on a show, so Coach would let them get away with doing some wild things. If one of them took a crazy-looking running hook shot, the other just had to try one, too. Dave would be shaking his head in disbelief but rarely said a word."

There were several bumps in the road during the 1972–73 campaign. The Friars, who were now playing their home games at the newly opened 12,400-seat Providence Civic Center, suffered their first road loss of the season to unranked Santa Clara, 97–92, on December 16. A month later, in a nationally televised game, top-ranked UCLA humbled No. 11 Providence, 101–77, at Pauley Pavilion. In the showdown against Walton, Barnes picked up two early fouls and was never a factor.

Not that the setback depressed Bad News for too long. Just a few hours after the game, he and several teammates took in a show at a seedy strip club on Hollywood Boulevard. A performer named "Black Velvet" was finishing her act when Barnes, attired in a silk cape and a fedora adorned with a foot-long white feather that curled upward, leaped onto the stage and carried the scantily clothed entertainer into her dressing room. Consolation prize in his arms, he did not return to the team hotel until seven o'clock the following morning.

Providence won 15 straight following the UCLA defeat, rolling into the NCAA tournament with a 24–2 record. The Friars handily beat St. Joseph's, 89–76, in their tourney opener. Penn, the team that had eliminated them the previous year, was next to be knocked out. Barnes was near-perfect in the 87–65 victory, scoring 20 points and grabbing 13 rebounds. His 10-for-10 shooting from the floor set an all-time tournament record for most field goal attempts without a miss.

In the Elite Eight, fifth-rated Providence faced tenth-ranked Maryland. The Terrapins, with a 23–6 mark, were coached by the boisterous Lefty Driesell, who had been trumpeting his team all season as the "UCLA of the East." At a pregame press conference, he managed to insult DiGregorio by referring to him as "that DiGrago, Digro kid, whatever his name is" and then adding, "Ah, just call him Number 15."

The Atlantic Coast Conference runners-up had a talent-laden starting lineup, with sophomore John Lucas at point, Tom McMillen at power forward, and Lenny Elmore at center. Lucas would go on to be the first overall pick of the 1976 NBA draft, while McMillen and Elmore would be selected ninth and thirteenth respectively in '74.

A three-point underdog, Maryland was demolished by Providence. DiGregorio led the way with 30 points, despite fouling out with eight minutes left in regulation. Stacom added 24. Barnes ruled the lanes, snatching 15 rebounds, one less than the combined total of McMillen and Elmore, in the 103–89 blowout that thrust Providence into the Final Four. After the game, a grinning DiGregorio told reporters, "Go ask Driesell if he knows how to say my name now."

"We're headed for a rematch against UCLA," Barnes said. "This time we're going to take care of business."

But first the Friars would have to get past the Memphis State Tigers, who were led by junior Larry Kenon, rated by many scouts as the second-best underclassman power forward pro prospect in the country, behind only Barnes.

With only the Tigers in their way, Providence jumped out to an early 24–16 lead in the Final Four matchup. DiGregorio was at his creative best, dribbling into the lane for five easy baskets. The floor general's highlight-reel moment came when he zipped a 35-foot behind-the-back pass between two befuddled defenders and into the hands of a wide-open Stacom, who caught the ball in stride and tossed in an uncontested layup. In the open court, Barnes sprinted past defenders to finish off three fastbreaks. Nat Holman, the legendary former CCNY coach who had won both the NCAA and NIT championships in 1950, called the Friars' fast start "the best eight minutes of basketball I've ever seen."

"We were running them into the ground," DiGregorio recalls. "Everything was going our way. And then it happened. Marvin went down."

While blocking a shot, which was ruled a goaltending violation, Barnes lost his balance and twisted his right knee, falling to the floor with a thud. After gingerly taking two steps, he was helped to the bench and sat out the remainder of the first half. Minus its inside scoring threat, Providence relied on DiGregorio's penetration and playmaking to hold a 49–40 advantage at intermission.

Barnes's absence, though, took its toll in the second half as Memphis State relentlessly jammed the ball inside to Kenon, who finished with 28 points and 22 rebounds. With 5:51 remaining and the Friars trailing 85–80, Barnes, his wounded knee heavily taped, reentered the game. For the next 1:47 of play, he limped up and down the court, grimacing with each tentative, stiff-legged step he took. Twenty seconds after putting in a flat-footed layup that cut the Memphis State lead to a single point, Barnes was taken out of the lineup by Gavitt. "Dave did the right thing. At that point, I was hurting the team because my knee had completely locked up. If I had stayed out there, we basically would've been playing four-on-five."

While Barnes watched forlornly from the bench, the Tigers put together a 13–1 surge to close out the game and come away with a 98–85 victory. (In the NCAA title matchup, UCLA crushed Memphis State, 87–66, as Walton connected on an astounding 21-of-22 field goal attempts.)

"Not making it to the championship game was a killer," said Barnes, who was named a third-team All-American by *The Sporting News* after having averaged 18.3 points and 19 rebounds for the season. "That rematch against UCLA would have been the greatest game ever played because both teams relied upon nonstop offense. Ask the PC fans who followed us that season and they'll swear we would have beaten UCLA, especially on a neutral court instead of at Pauley Pavilion. I think we would have torn them apart. No, check that, I know we would've."

Walton naturally disagrees. "Marvin, Ernie, and Kevin were tremendous players. But that's all tiny Providence College had for talent. We were the mighty Bruins, who went 30–0 for the second straight year. We had subs on our team who were drafted by the pros. It's what you call depth, something the Friars definitely did not have. Just look at what happened to them after Barnes got injured against Memphis. They folded. Marvin should have been thankful we didn't play them in the championship game. That injury of his saved them from the utter embarrassment of getting buried by us—again."

In a postgame press release, the Providence team physician termed the damage to Barnes's knee as "a moderate strain." But when

X-rays revealed that the Friars center had suffered a slight carti-
lage tear and a dislocated kneecap, it was feared surgery might be
required.

After conferring with three prominent orthopedic specialists,
Gavitt told his hobbled pro prospect, "I want you to take three
months off before hitting the weights to build up the muscles
around the knee. Then we'll see if the doctors believe an operation
is necessary."

For two and a half months, Barnes wore a cast to keep his
knee stabilized and then resumed workouts in late May. "I was
running at full speed. There was a little swelling, but I could live
with that. I wanted no part of surgery because I didn't want the
pro scouts to think I might be damaged goods."

The recuperating center offered a unique theory to teammates
as to why his knee had buckled. "It was because of the damned
three-inch high-heeled pimp shoes I wore all season. When I tried
to walk and keep my balance in those things, my knees shook.
Pretty soon, they felt sore. Right then and there, I should have
thrown those stupid shoes away, but I just couldn't. I thought I
looked so cool wearing them that I was willing to put up with a
little discomfort. You know, I was styling for my women."

In the offseason, the Rockets selected Barnes in the first round
of the ABA undergraduate draft and upped their previous bid of
$300,000 for two seasons to a guaranteed $1 million over five
years. The proposal was tempting, and Woolf was pressuring the
twenty-one-year-old to sign. Gavitt, however, reminded his star
of their conversation eight months earlier. "I told you that this
past season would be Ernie's time to get all the publicity and
praise. I came through for him, didn't I? For a point guard to end
up being taken third overall [by the Buffalo Braves] in the NBA
draft, that was something special. I'll come through for you, too.

I promise that if you stay for your senior year, you'll end up with a far better offer than the one you've got now."

It was a quick and easy sell. Barnes picked up the phone in the athletic office, called Denver Head Coach Alex Hannum, and said he would welcome the chance to play for him, but only after the 1973–74 college season.

Despite DiGregorio's departure to the NBA, the Friars were ranked among the nation's top-ten teams for almost the entire 1973–74 season. In the team's fourth game, Barnes scored a school-record 52 points in a 94–92 win over Austin Peay at the Civic Center. Matched against Percy Howard, who would go on to catch a touchdown pass for the Dallas Cowboys in Super Bowl X, he overpowered his 6-foot-4 opponent and converted 23 field goals, also a Providence record.

As the Friars continued to win impressively, the senior co-captain became quite the comedic entertainer. Minutes before a home game against William & Mary on December 20, he gallantly escorted four of his most devoted girlfriends to front-row seats behind the basket nearest to the team's bench. From the opening tipoff, he hot-dogged for the enthralled troupe, performing the Ali Shuffle in the lane while looking over his shoulder and hollering, "I am the greatest." With Providence up by 28 late in the game, the court jester rooster-strutted his way over to his personal rooting section and shouted, "Hey, ladies, how's News looking?"

Such wacky stunts genuinely amused Gavitt, who had become a father figure to his whimsical superstar.

Facing the University of Massachusetts on the road in mid-January, Providence trailed 76–75 with less than 20 seconds remaining. The Minutemen were in possession of the ball and Gavitt, shouting from the bench, ordered his players to intentionally foul point guard Rick Pitino, a feisty, hot-headed 6-foot senior who was a mediocre free throw shooter. Stepping to the line, the future Hall of Fame coach bounced the ball four times, took a deep breath, and bricked the front end of a one-and-one. The Friars capitalized on the miss, corralling the rebound and racing upcourt. With 00:06 showing on the game clock, Stacom banked in an 18-foot jumper that lifted PC to a 77–76 victory. Leaving the court, a jubilant Barnes called out to Pitino, "Hey, squirt, I'm sending you a Providence jersey because you damn well were our MVP tonight."

When the team entered the Palestra in Philadelphia for a game against St. Joseph's two days later, Barnes seemed mesmerized as he watched several opposition players use a contraption that propelled basketballs off a backboard from varying angles. "Hey, coach, maybe we should get one of those," he suggested. Without a second's pause, Gavitt shot back, "Marvin, we've already got a rebounding machine—you."

Nothing flustered the tenacious center during a close game. In a February contest at St. Bonaventure, the student body section broke into a deafening chant of "tire iron, tire iron" every time Barnes touched the ball. Trailing 67–62 late in the second half, the Friars called a timeout. As the team huddled up, Barnes stared at some of the more demonstrative hecklers and shouted, "I hear you. Now just sit back, shut up, and watch me work." Over the closing three and a half minutes, he recorded nine points, five rebounds, and two blocks as Providence pulled in front and held on for a 74–69 victory. In 32 minutes of playing time, Barnes totaled 29 points, 16 rebounds, and four blocks, much to the displeasure of the Bonnies' raucous peanut gallery.

Heading into the NCAA tournament, the Friars were 22–3, but they were sent home early. After beating Penn in the First Round, 84–69, the Friars were crushed by the eventual national champion North Carolina State, 92–78, in their Sweet Sixteen match-up as guard David "Skywalker" Thompson poured in 40 points.

For the season, Barnes averaged 22.1 points and led the nation in rebounding with 18.7 a game, earning him first-team All-American honors from UPI, AP, *Basketball Weekly*, *Basketball Digest*, and *The Sporting News*.

As the NBA draft neared, Rhode Island's favorite son was constantly coming up with one-liners to provide the media with snippets of levity. One off-the-cuff remark, though, did not endear him to the blue-collar fans who had been in his corner. On Commencement Day at Providence, Barnes, who had been handed a blank diploma because he was ten credits shy of his degree, was asked by a reporter what his fair market value as a pro should be. "I won't play for less than a million," he boldly answered. "I'd rather work in a factory than take less than that."

The flippant comment was designed to get a cheap laugh. Instead it went national, sparking outrage about bratty, money-hungry athletes and their high-and-mighty attitudes toward the average US worker, whose annual salary in 1974 was $8,030. As writer Scoop Jackson would note years later in *Slam* magazine, "Marvin Barnes was the original Negro with an ego, an athlete whom America wasn't ready for."

Eight

A FREE SPIRIT
AND THE BIG BAD WOOLF

Bill Walton, UCLA's hippie-in-residence and the only three-time Player of the Year in NCAA history, was the jackpot prize of the 1974 NBA draft. So when the Portland Trail Blazers won a coin flip with the Philadelphia 76ers for the first overall pick, Big Red was headed to the Rose City. Barnes was then selected by the Sixers.

"Those two are in a class of their own," Dr. Jack Ramsay, who was coaching the Buffalo Braves, said at the time. "There are other talented players in the draft, but, quite honestly, Walton and Barnes are the only ones you can build a team around."

Barnes's ABA rights were still held by the Denver franchise, which had been rechristened the Nuggets, but the league had worked out an arrangement that allowed any of its clubs to sign the Providence All-American. Its board of governors had ruled that if a team other than Denver were to reach a contractual agreement with Barnes, the Nuggets, as compensation, would be awarded the first overall selection in the 1975 draft, which turned out to be 7-foot-1 Marvin "The Human Eraser" Webster.

Gavitt urged his center to hire Attorney Larry Fleischer as his representative. "I knew Dave had no use for Woolf," Barnes said. "He had seen the two of us talking before a few games, and I could see he was steamed. Maybe he had a hunch that Bob was throwing some cash my way. Who knows?"

Despite all the "favors" Woolf had done for him, the consensus All-American heeded his coach's advice and chose Fleischer, who was the Players' Association general counsel, as well as the agent for DiGregorio, who had just been voted the NBA's Rookie of the Year. Barnes, though, frustrated with what he perceived was a lack of progress in contract talks with the 76ers, fired the New York–based dealmaker fifteen days after the draft and reunited with Woolf.

Philadelphia was in dire need of both scoring and rebounding, placing Barnes in the position to be a franchise savior. He, however, never seriously considered signing with the Sixers because, according to what Woolf had told him, they were only offering a half-guaranteed four-year deal worth a total of $900,000. Throw in the fact that Walton's five-year, $3 million contract with Portland was fully guaranteed, and, well, Marvin felt insulted.

The 76ers denied such a lowball proposal was ever made.

"Barnes was completely misled by Woolf," says Gene Shue, who was Philadelphia's general manager in 1974. "The year before we had paid Doug Collins, the top pick in the draft, $1.4 million for five years, all guaranteed—and he was a guard, not a big man. We needed Marvin in the worst way, and we were willing to pay him top dollar. We had to get a high-scoring frontcourt player who could help boost attendance because we had won only 25 games the previous season. You don't use the second overall pick on a player you don't feel is going to be a perennial All-Star, and you don't draft a guy that high unless you're going to do everything possible to sign him."

Shue claims that Philly's initial offer was a 75-percent guaranteed $1.1 million for four years, plus performance incentives for rebounding and scoring. "I thought it was an excellent starting point," he says. "Woolf told me he'd get back to me with a counter-proposal. That's how good-faith bargaining works. But he never called me again. I had heard plenty of stories about agents getting kickbacks from the ABA to steer their clients to its teams. From my experience with Woolf, I think those stories just might have been true."

Woolf told Barnes that his best move financially would be to sign with the ABA's Spirits of St. Louis. The team had been born in July of '74 after Ozzie and Danny Silna, two wealthy brothers from New Jersey who had made their fortune manufacturing polyester fabrics, bought the Carolina Cougars for $1.5 million and immediately relocated the franchise to the Gateway City. Prior to the sale, though, Cougars owner Tedd Munchak had stripped down the team, selling off the contracts of his two All-Star guards, Mack Calvin and Ted McClain. In addition, Carolina had also lost high-scoring small forward Billy Cunningham to free agency.

"When we started operations, we had just four veterans under contract, and only two of them, Joe Caldwell and Steve Jones, were potential starters," said Harry Weltman, who was the Spirits general manager. "We had the rights to two very promising rookie forwards in Maurice Lucas and Gus Gerard, but to be truly competitive we had to add at least two more players who could come in and be major contributors. Trouble was I didn't have the ability to make any deals because no one on our roster had much trade value."

For St. Louis, signing Barnes wasn't just a hope, it was a necessity. "We knew we had to acquire one guy with superstar qualities who could give us instant credibility and also help us establish a solid fan base," Weltman said. "I thought if we could somehow find a way to get Marvin, we'd solve our two greatest problems."

During a conference call, Ozzie Silna, the Spirits' principal owner, told Barnes, "We may be in our first year, but we've got a young, hungry group of guys. If you sign with us, you'll be the cornerstone of the franchise."

The flattery worked to perfection.

Woolf and Barnes flew to New York to meet with Weltman and the team's legal counsel, Donald Schupak. As the negotiating session was about to begin, Woolf told his client to wait in the reception area of Schupak's office. "My future was at stake. I felt like I had every right to be in that meeting," Barnes would say later. "After a while, I got tired of sitting by myself, with nothing but the *Financial Times* and *Wall Street Journal* to read. I was ready to walk out the door and head back to Providence."

After two hours of bargaining, it seemed as if a deal was imminent. Woolf emerged from the meeting and revealed to Barnes that St. Louis was offering a total of $2.2 million for seven years, which included a $100,000 signing bonus, $35,000 for a down payment on a house or condo, and a new Cadillac Fleetwood.

What the crafty agent failed to mention initially was that the salary package would be spread over fourteen years, which meant the "can't-miss" center/forward would be receiving only $150,000 annually—and that was before taxes. When finally informed of the $1.05 million in deferred payments, Barnes balked. "Hell no! What if the league folds in a year or two, which I hear is very possible? What if every owner files for bankruptcy? Then who's going to pay me all the money I supposedly should be getting until I'm thirty-six fucking years old?" All his concerns were valid.

Woolf, however, was able to persuade his client to accept the terms, maintaining that the deferred compensation would limit the amount of money former Providence teammate Larry Ketvirtis could be awarded if he were to win his civil court lawsuit. Barnes later claimed that Schupak also gave him a verbal commitment that the contract's payment schedule would be restructured once the anticipated "tire iron" case had been resolved.

As part of the contract, which did not include an injury protection clause or any incentives, the Spirits agreed to pay Woolf's 10-percent commission, which amounted to $220,000, up front. Barnes, though, would be obligated to reimburse the team $20,000 per year until the lawyer's fee was fully repaid.

"There were some agents who were nothing but whores. They would sell their mothers for a deal," sports attorney Ron Grinker told author Terry Pluto. "It was not uncommon for an agent to be paid more in the first year of a contract than what the player would receive. . . . It was just robbery."

Before signing, Barnes wondered why someone as cagey as Woolf hadn't contacted the 76ers to seek a counter-offer that would be competitive. "I kept waiting for him to call Shue and find out if he would at least be willing to come close to what St. Louis was offering, but Bob never did."

An hour after the Spirits contract had been finalized, Shue was informed by a Philadelphia reporter that his top draft pick had agreed to terms with St. Louis. "When I heard the news, I knew we had a crisis on our hands. There was no way to avoid going through another disastrous season. It wasn't until we were able to acquire [free agent forward] George McGinnis in '75 that we finally had a consistent inside scoring threat. A year after that, we bought Julius Erving's contract from the Nets. That's when we became a legitimate playoff team.

"Had Marvin signed with us in '74, I honestly don't know if we could have gone after Dr. J in '76. I can tell you this: We wouldn't have paid as much as we did [$3 million] to the Nets for his rights. Not that we didn't absolutely love everything about Erving's game, it's just that I don't see any way we could have afforded to pay Barnes and McGinnis, as well as forking over such a huge amount to buy Julius's contract, along with paying him his $800,000 annual salary.

"Woolf called me a month after the whole debacle. I told my secretary to let him know I was busy—for the next twenty years."

Two weeks after officially becoming a Spirit, Barnes was summoned to appear in federal district court in Providence as the defendant in a $1.5 million civil suit filed by Ketvirtis.

"No surprise to me," the suddenly well-to-do pro athlete said. "The only shocking thing is that he's not going after the whole $2.2 million I'll be getting from St. Louis."

Unlike in the criminal case, Barnes had no doubts he would be able to prove he was innocent of striking his former college teammate with a tire iron. When Ketvirtis took the stand, lead defense attorney Robert Conason grilled him about whether he considered himself an out-of-control "dirty player."

> **Question:** "Did you have any fights at George Washington University before transferring to Providence?"
> **Answer:** "I recall one incident when I nudged this other fellow from behind. He turned around and hit me, and I started to fight."

> **Question:** "Did Providence teammate Ray Johnson make complaints to you about your play?"
> **Answer:** "He might have."

> **Question:** "Anybody else make complaints?"
> **Answer:** "I think Dave Gavitt may have spoken to me."

Question: "In your first year on the Providence varsity, did the players complain there was a danger of injury because of your style of play?"

Answer: "I think there was some talk, yes."

Question: "Were some teammates injured by contact from you?"

Answer: "Yeah, there were some."

Question: "Some of them had to go to the hospital, correct?"

Answer: "Yes, they did."

Question: "Do you remember an incident against Southern California shown on national TV?"

Answer: "Yes. Ron Riley of Southern Cal gave me an elbow and then a quick punch. I think I tried to punch him, but I was already falling back."

Question: "You never tried to hit him again in the game?"

Answer: "I wouldn't say I never tried to hit him, but I didn't throw a punch at him."

Question: "Were there times when you swung punches at your own teammates during scrimmages?"

Answer: "I can recall one specific punch thrown at Franny Costello, a forward."

Question: "Did you have a fight where you chased one of your teammates, Nehru King?"

Answer: "Yes.

Question: "Did you state at a pretrial hearing that you thought specific players were out to get you?"

Answer: "Basically I thought it was the black athletic group."

In effect, Ketvirtis had been all but damned by his own words.

The medical experts' testimony was also compelling. Two respected physicians stated that all the evidence, including the X-rays taken at Carney Hospital where Ketvirtis initially had been examined, supported Barnes's claim that he had never hit his teammate with anything but his fist. One of the doctors, Dr. Charles Mandell, head of the Fall River, Massachusetts, Hospital radiology department, told the media after the trial that he believed Barnes's acceptance of a plea deal in the criminal case had been a "terrible error in judgment because there was no possibility a jury could have ignored all the medical facts that backed up his account of the incident."

Arguably, the most dramatic moment of the civil trial came when Ketvirtis admitted that had Barnes been dismissed from the PC basketball team, he might have considered dropping the whole matter.

"All along, Larry was figuring that if I got kicked off the team, he'd get his chance to be a big star," Barnes said. "My only thought while he was testifying was: 'What a little bitch.' All he really wanted was to get me thrown off so he could steal my minutes."

Because Barnes acknowledged he had landed a punch during the assault, $10,000 was awarded to Ketvirtis for the cost of his medical bills. The jury, however, did not see fit to grant the plaintiff a penny of the $1.49 million he had been seeking in punitive damages. As the panel's foreman, Anthony Lucca, told reporters, "To us, it was clear from all the testimony and evidence that the injuries were from a punch."

Despite the favorable outcome, Barnes would forever be tagged "Tire Iron."

"Even today, there are people who ask for my autograph, and want me to sign it 'Tire Iron,'" he would say decades later. "They have the grapes to tell me it'll make their friends laugh. Well, it doesn't make me laugh. Call me News or, better yet, just plain Marvin. That works just fine for me."

Once Barnes had received his $100,000 signing bonus from the Spirits, it took him less than three months to fritter away the entire sum.

After repaying Woolf $42,000 for the loans he and his mother had accepted during his college days, the big spender bought his sister a new car and paid for four of his friends to tag along with him on a ten-day trip to Hawaii.

For Bad News, suddenly flush with more money than he could have ever imagined, it was essential to look the part of the young, successful millionaire athlete. Accordingly, he shelled out $10,000 for a new wardrobe and dropped another $16,000 on a down payment for a pre-owned 1965 Rolls Royce while also keeping his new white Caddy "to use when it's raining."

Days before the Spirits training camp was scheduled to get underway, Woolf phoned his client to discuss an urgent matter. "Marvin, I've been reviewing all your bills that have come into my office. We need to put you on a tight budget. As of today, you're almost $20,000 in debt."

To owe such a staggering amount was incomprehensible for Barnes. "Bob, I haven't even played my first pro game, and you're telling me I'm twenty grand in the hole? Why didn't you warn me before I went out and blew my entire signing bonus?"

"Because you were determined to splurge," Woolf replied. "You're an intelligent guy. You had to know you were spending a great deal of money. I didn't think I needed to explain that to you."

"But you're supposed to be my financial adviser," Barnes shot back. "It's your job to make sure I'm doing OK moneywise. If I owed, say, a couple thousand, I could get a loan to hold me over until my first paycheck, but coming up with twenty grand, that's impossible. You're the business expert. I'm just a twenty-two-year-old kid who likes to have a good time. . . . It's over, Bob.

I'm firing your ass." Marvin slammed down the phone and never again spoke to the sports attorney, who had already pocketed his $220,000 fee for negotiating the Spirits contract.

In 1976, Woolf wrote a book, *Behind Closed Doors*, in which he detailed his successful career in sports law. An entire chapter was devoted to his dealings with Barnes, who was portrayed as being undisciplined, uninformed, and unintelligent.

"I know there are people who are going to believe all the tall tales he spun in that book," Marvin said. "I admit that a few of his stories about my spending habits were true, but most of them were written to make it seem like he was doing his best to watch out for my interests. He made it sound like I ignored all his so-called words of wisdom. Fact is Bob Woolf didn't give me one bit of decent advice. I got played. I got hustled. The man was nothing but a slick fraud who enjoyed being in the spotlight with the rich and famous. I still remember when I was a senior at PC, and he took me to a Celtics game. The man paraded me around Boston Garden like I was one of them prized purebreds that are led around on a leash at a dog show."

Barnes was not the only pro athlete who came to detest Woolf's ethics. Boston Bruins star center Derek Sanderson, who signed a contract with sports attorney in 1967, found out far too late that Woolf had taken advantage of him financially in several business ventures.

"I was just a naive twenty-year-old. I trusted the guy and gave him power of attorney, which was my big mistake," says Sanderson, who became an alcoholic during his playing days. "By the time I learned how he had been misusing my money, the guy had fleeced me out of a hundred thousand bucks, maybe more, through a couple of investment scams.

"When I signed my record $2.6 million contract with the Philadelphia Blazers of the World Hockey Association in '72,

Woolf charged me 10 percent, and he also blackmailed the team's owners into giving him another 10 percent for brokering the deal. Shit, he made $520,000. I was just twenty-six, and I didn't have a clue about what he was up to. It was a classic case of double-dipping, something a reputable agent would never do."

In 1989, NBA stars Robert Parish, Sean Elliott, Glen Rice, and Darrell Griffith all sued Woolf for receiving his commissions up front instead of following collective bargaining rules that prohibited agents from collecting fees until their clients actually were paid their salaries. When the specifics of the lawsuit hit the newspapers, Woolf, who would pass away from a heart attack in 1993, quickly and quietly settled with the players, thus avoiding further negative publicity.

"With that toothy fake smile of his," Barnes said, "Bob Woolf conned a lot of people. I should know because he damn near bankrupted me."

Nine

THE ROOKIE EXPERIENCE: COMEDY AND CHAOS

At a press conference to formally announce his signing with the Spirits, Barnes wore a bright yellow construction worker's hard hat—this from a guy who a few months earlier said he'd rather work in a factory than play for less than $1 million. "Right away," team owner Ozzie Silna said years later, "we knew we were dealing with a different breed of cat."

The media soon gravitated to the opinionated first-year pro whose spontaneous remarks earned him a reputation of being the ultimate quote machine. All a reporter had to do was insert the "Barnes Bombshell of the Day" into an article about the Spirits and it became must-read material. At times, it seemed Bad News was intentionally inviting trouble by expressing his candid views. For example, when asked how conservative Missourians might view his rather gaudy way of life, he answered, "There are people around here who don't relate well to that type of Negro."

Teammates were thoroughly entertained by Barnes's animated banter with the press. "He was more outrageous than Charles Barkley," declares guard Steve "Snapper" Jones. "He loved to see his name in the newspapers and his face on TV. He always spoke his mind, and he didn't care whether anyone agreed with him. Most of us thought some of his comments had to be put-ons, but I don't think anyone really knew for sure."

On media day, reporters swarmed around the loose-tongued face of the franchise, hoping he'd dish out a few juicy tidbits. As the lively group interview was about to conclude, the Spirits' self-appointed spokesman spotted a short white kid wearing a madras sports jacket and looking as if he were playing hooky from high school as he eavesdropped from 10 feet away.

"I didn't know why this young guy was there," Barnes said years later, "but he seemed scared to death. I was curious, so I went over to him and said, 'Hey, I'm Marvin. What's your name, big fella?'"

"I'm Bob, Bob Costas," the baby-faced onlooker said. "I'll be doing the play-by-play on KMOX. Pleasure to meet you.'"

Marvin put an arm around the twenty-two-year-old sportscaster, fresh out of Syracuse University, and said, "Got a deal for you, Bob. You make me sound good on the radio, and I'll always have your back."

Costas made everyone sound good. "He usually did his broadcasts at St. Louis Arena from right next to our bench, and I'd listen in on him when I came out of the game for a rest," Barnes said. "Bob had style, just like me. He was smooth and confident. I'd kid him all the time that he'd be going 'big-time' on us in a year or two. And that's just what happened. He's been the best in the business for decades." (Over the course of his career, the NBC commentator has won twenty-six Emmys and been voted Sports Broadcaster of the Year a record eight times.)

On the first day of practice, Spirits Head Coach Bob MacKinnon, who had been an assistant with the NBA's Buffalo Braves the previous three seasons, informed his prized rookie that he wanted him to take between 20 and 25 shots a game. Barnes, figuring he would make at least half of his attempts, thought the strategy made perfect sense.

MacKinnon's calm demeanor had a positive effect on his hyperactive whiz kid—at least in the beginning. When St. Louis faced the San Diego Conquistadors for the first time on October 29, the coach made a point of casually mentioning in his pre-game pep talk that Caldwell Jones, the opposition's center, was the league's best defender. Barnes, responding to the thinly veiled challenge, proceeded to torch the 6-foot-11 Jones for 48 points and 30 rebounds.

"If I had known I was going to be this good," Marvin told reporters following the game, "I'd have asked Ozzie Silna for a lot more money."

For the first month of the season, the Sprits' inside force was among the league's top ten in points, rebounds, and blocked shots. The team, although playing sub-.500 ball, was starting to show signs of jelling . . . until Bad News vanished without a trace.

The strange saga began when "Pogo" Joe Caldwell, the team's player representative, scolded Barnes for being naive. "Your contract is a total joke," the thirty-three-year-old veteran barked. "You're our big gun, our MVP. Five players on this team have injury clauses, and you're not one of them."

Now believing he had been snookered by management, the impulsive rookie hired Caldwell's representative, Marshall Boyer, an eccentric wheeler dealer from Los Angeles, to renegotiate his deal. The agent, who claimed to have cosmic rays running through his body and often spoke in nonsensical riddles, took immediate and drastic action, persuading his new client to go into hiding—at a billiards tournament in Ohio. For four days, the team didn't have any knowledge as to the whereabouts of its highest-salaried player until *Dayton Journal Herald* sports reporter Mark Purdy received a tip that the dispirited Spirit was playing eight ball in a smoke-filled pool hall and subsequently interviewed the St. Louis sensation about his one-man strike. Meanwhile, Boyer seemed to be stumped as to what his next move might be.

After consulting with his mother, Barnes severed ties with the oddball adviser and moved on to Irwin Weiner, a former high school dropout who represented Knicks All-Star guard Walt "Clyde" Frazier and Julius Erving. Weiner's plan of attack was to somehow reach a settlement with the Silna brothers to release their disgruntled star. Once that had been accomplished, he would then negotiate a multimillion-dollar contract with an NBA club for his client's services. The AWOL Spirit, however, didn't buy into the farfetched strategy, dismissing his latest mouthpiece two days after he had signed on with him.

At that point, Lula intervened. She phoned Ozzie Silna and received a commitment that he would help straighten out her son's mounting financial problems, but only if he would return to St. Louis immediately and honor his contract. "You're doing all the wrong things," she told Marvin. "Don't blame the team for problems you brought upon yourself by listening to Bob Woolf and agreeing to a deal that you didn't believe was fair in the first place."

Heeding her wishes, Barnes rejoined the Spirits, who had lost three of four games during his absence. "And [Silna] told my mother that they would work my contract out with me. Of course I'm a momma's boy, so I said okay."

As a peace offering, Silna agreed to add an injury protection clause to the rookie's contract. He, however, refused to restructure the fourteen-year payout arrangement.

At the same time as St. Louis's prodigal son was practicing for the first time in eleven days, Caldwell was being suspended indefinitely because, according to management, he had "led Barnes astray." But as Costas later quipped, "Marvin spent much of his entire life 'astray.' He didn't need a map or someone to lead him there."

Pogo Joe, who averaged 16.1 points during his combined 11-year NBA/ABA career, would never play another game for St. Louis or any other pro team, having been blackballed for allegedly being a divisive clubhouse lawyer.

Unlike Caldwell, Barnes was free to resume his normal routine—at least "normal" by Marvin's standards. Days after returning to the Spirits, he arrived 45 minutes late for practice, insisting he was a guiltless victim of circumstances.

"My car conked out five miles from the arena," he explained. "It took a mechanic a good half-hour to fix it."

"But aren't you driving a Rolls Royce?" MacKinnon asked.

"Yeah, but they don't make 'em like they used to," Barnes deadpanned.

"OK, if you say so, Marvin," the unruffled coach replied, "but I don't think the Rolls people make too many lemons."

In early January, Costas missed the team flight to Memphis for a Spirits–Sounds game and didn't arrive at Mid-South Coliseum until midway through the first quarter. In his absence, the radio broadcast back to St. Louis was silent, except for the muffled sound of the public address announcer calling out the last name of the player who just scored. Upon taking his seat at courtside, the frazzled sportscaster, sweat beading across his forehead, feared he might lose his job.

At halftime, one of the Spirits asked the distraught play-by-play man how much money he would be fined. "In my business," Costas said, "they don't fine people for showing up late to a game. They fire them."

"Don't worry, Bob, they ain't going to can you," Barnes interrupted. "I'm going to put in a good word for you. I got a lot of pull around here. By now you've got to know that me and Ozzie Silna are tight. [Bear in mind that these statements seemed to be quite a stretch since they were coming out of the mouth of a player who had just skipped out on his team for eleven days.]

"Listen, even if they do dump your ass, you can come and work for me," Barnes kidded. "I've been looking for a little white dude to drive me around town in my Rolls. I'll get you one of those cool-looking chauffeur's caps, and I'll pay you good money, too."

Costas still enjoys recounting his most humorous Bad News anecdote:

The Spirits were flying from St. Louis to Louisville to play the Colonels on December 4. Barnes checked the itinerary and noticed that the return flight the next morning was scheduled to depart at 8 a.m. Its arrival time was listed as 7:58 a.m.

Bad News was perplexed and in full panic mode.

"This ain't right," he told Costas. "This says we're arriving in St. Louis two minutes before we even take off from Louisville."

"Yeah, it's correct," the broadcaster informed the visibly rattled player. "We're going from Eastern to Central Time. We gain an hour."

"Bro, bro, I don't know about you," Barnes replied, "but I ain't getting on no time machine." (Eventually, he "courageously" tempted fate and boarded the team flight back home.)

Following a lifeless 120–101 Spirits loss to the Nets in New York on March 7, Barnes stood in the lobby of the team's hotel and loudly announced to his teammates that it was time to "party hardy." A minute later, he invited two attractive basketball groupies to frolic the night away in his room even though the team had to catch a 7:15 a.m. flight to Norfolk, Virginia, the next morning for a game against the Squires.

When Barnes failed to show up for the 5:30 a.m. bus ride to LaGuardia Airport, team trainer Mike Kostich was dispatched to rouse the tardy star. Responding to a series of loud knocks at his door, Bad News, looking extremely hung over and fatigued, told Kostich he would make his own travel arrangements. By the time he arrived at LaGuardia five hours later, however, there were no more commercial departures to Norfolk that day. His only option would be to charter a private plane for himself and his two new girlfriends.

An airline employee introduced him to a pilot who offered to fly the trio to Norfolk for $1,500. The terms seemed reasonable, but there was a major hitch: Barnes had only $40 in his wallet and was not carrying any credit cards or checks.

To convince the pilot that he was indeed a man of financial means, the fast-thinking rookie reached into his travel bag and produced a copy of his recently signed $5,000 Topps basketball card contract. A deal was quickly struck. Barnes promised the self-employed aviator a front-row seat to the game, along with an autographed basketball, and said he'd "order" the Spirits general manager to pay for the flight as soon as they arrived at the arena.

With less than hour remaining before game time, the six-seat prop plane touched down in Norfolk. Ducking into one of the airport restrooms, "Movin' Marvin," as St. Louis Director of Operations Rudy Martzke had nicknamed him, changed into his uniform and donned a full-length fur coat. Then the traveling party squeezed into a taxi and headed to the Scope, home of the Squires. Two blocks from the arena, the cabbie was told to pull into a McDonald's where a takeout order was placed for fifteen cheeseburgers, six large fries, and five grape sodas.

Making his grand entrance at courtside, Barnes, with his female companions clinging to his arms, spotted Harry Weltman, who seemed to be a tad testy, and nonchalantly approached him. Before the Spirits GM could utter a word, mink-wrapped Marvin reached into one of the McDonald's bags and handed his boss the 1974 equivalent of a Happy Meal. "Harry, I got good news and bad news for you. The good news is the food is on me," the seemingly oblivious center said. "The bad news is that you owe my pilot $1,500 for the plane ride, plus the twenty-five bucks he shelled out for our cab ride. Take it out of my next check."

"[Weltman] is pissed off, but, they gotta pay the pilot, or I'm going to jail," Barnes said with a smile.

"I was literally speechless because tipoff was only ten minutes away, and there was Marvin joking around and wearing that ridiculous fur of his," Weltman said later. "Don't ask me why, but I wrote out a check and paid the pilot."

MacKinnon was in a far less forgiving mood. After the unapologetic last-minute arrival had breezed into the locker room and shouted, "Have no fear, News is here," the apoplectic coach muttered a few unflattering words and told the cheeseburger-munching rules breaker that he was being yanked from the starting lineup.

"Coach was more pissed than I had ever seen him," Gerard said years later, "but we [the players] actually thought it was kind of cool that Marvin had chartered his own plane. I mean this was the seventies, and doing something that wild and that expensive was unheard of."

With the St. Louis trailing by 12 halfway through the first quarter, a simmering MacKinnon looked the down bench and yelled, "Barnes, go in there and make something happen. Earn your money for a change."

And Bad News did just that. Almost every one of his jumpers dropped straight through the net. "I could have shot lefty with my eyes closed and wouldn't have missed," he said years later. "I'd run up the court and shout out to one of my girls, 'This one's for you, baby.' Next trip down, I'd look over at the other one and yell, 'Here comes a couple points just for you, sweetheart.'"

Playing 41 minutes, Barnes finished with 43 points, 19 rebounds, and three blocked shots as St. Louis rallied to beat Virginia, 114–111.

"There's no denying that he was sensational in that game," Weltman said, "but I told Silna the next day that we should still fine him at least a couple thousand. My recommendation was totally ignored. I think from that moment on, Marvin felt he could get away with doing whatever he pleased. His teammates started joking that he must be blackmailing Silna because he knew some deep, dark secret about the man's past. Players would complain to me all the time about Marvin's selfish behavior, and I couldn't give them any kind of explanation for why he was always given special treatment. All I know is that he made everyone in the front office look like saps."

Jones, for one, thought it was a disgrace that management turned a blind eye to the rookie's irresponsible acts. "After the All-Star break, Barnes became more and more undependable," the former St. Louis guard says. "He hated to practice, was always late for the team bus, and started dogging it when we were losing badly. Even though the owners always told the media that he had been disciplined for his conduct, I don't think they ever made him pay a nickel of his so-called fines. He was like the class clown in grade school, always trying to see how much he could get away with before the teacher would pull him by the ear and punish him."

Barnes was well aware of the growing criticism by teammates. Quite obviously, he didn't care. When it came to abiding by team rules, the Spirits' agitator publicly declared himself a conscientious objector. "I don't want to act like an old man of thirty when I'm only twenty-two," he pontificated to reporters as they furiously scribbled down his pseudo rant. "But they keep telling me, 'You can't make any more mistakes, Marvin. Don't miss any more planes, Marvin. Be on time, Marvin. Drink your milk, Marvin. Eat your vegetables, Marvin.' Man, I'm twenty-two, and a twenty-two-year-old kid ain't no genius. I'm tired of being 'the franchise.'"

Ten

PUTTING THE "FUN" IN DYSFUNCTIONAL

Indiana Pacers forward George McGinnis, who shared 1975 MVP honors with Julius Erving, once described the Spirits of St. Louis as a team that "led the world in crazies." His harsh assessment went unchallenged, principally because the first-year club had the unmanageable "Bad News" Barnes and his equally flaky rookie sidekick, James "Fly" Williams, on its roster.

A New York City schoolyard phenom, the 6-foot-5 Williams had averaged 28 points during his two varsity seasons at Austin Peay before turning pro at age twenty-one. "He was a likeable and talented kid, but he always wanted to do things on his own terms," Weltman said. "His priority was to be a master showman on the court, so he'd do anything to be the center of attention. I remember one time when we were on a fastbreak and Fly was trailing the play. All of a sudden he stopped running, casually walked over to the courtside seats, grabbed a cup of beer out of some poor woman's hand, chugged it down, and strolled back onto the court."

Williams was a streak shooter who judged his success on the basis of how many field goals he attempted in a game. "Twenty minutes, 15 shots," he told teammates. "Ten minutes, ten shots. Just get me the rock and I be bringing us home."

The one-on-one specialist had no upper front teeth and spoke with a slight lisp. The team offered to pay for him to get a denture plate, but he refused. "Can't do it," he said. "I'd lose all my personality. I wouldn't be 'The Fly' no more."

A native of Brooklyn, Williams often entertained his many female friends at his townhouse on off days. "Fly had them cooking his meals, washing his car, running errands, the whole nine yards," Barnes said. "While they were busy doing their chores, he'd be snorting coke. He's the guy who first got me into using on a regular basis. Until I started hanging with him, I had hardly touched the stuff."

On the night before many home games, Bad News would go club-hopping with the visiting team's best players. "I'd show them all a real good time. Then I'd drive them back to their hotel and send up a couple of attractive hookers—I mean knockouts—to their rooms. I wanted the girls to take care of business. I told them to drain the guys, keep 'em up all night. I was hoping that when these suckers, all first-team All-Stars, showed up at the arena the next night, they'd all be legless. Funny thing is my plan never worked."

At the opposite end of the spectrum, from the madcap world of Barnes and Williams was serious-minded power forward Maurice Lucas, a dedicated practitioner of yoga. The square-jawed rookie who had starred at Marquette would go on to become one of the most feared enforcers in the NBA, but he was far from a rugged intimidator when he entered the pro ranks. "In training camp, Mo was soft as cotton," said Barnes. "I toughened him up by using every dirty trick in the book when I went up against him in practice. I'd kick the living crap out of him, and he'd never come back at me. He played scared."

Lucas, who died in 2010 after courageously battling cancer, was a man of few words. "Marvin was your typical hit-and-run type," he said years later, responding to his former teammate's criticism. "You know, he'd cheapshot you when you weren't looking and run away before you could retaliate. I'll say this much about him: He always *talked* a good game."

While Barnes and Williams were mentally "out there," there was one member of the Spirits who was a "closet crazy." Gus Gerard, a quiet, twenty-one-year-old small forward who had been signed to a five-year $950,000 contract by St. Louis following his junior year at the University of Virginia, was considered a positive influence in the locker room, a dedicated, hard-nosed type who was well respected by teammates, the coaching staff, and the front office.

What no one realized, however, was that the 6-foot-8 starter, who averaged 15.7 points and 7.9 rebounds in 1974–75 and was voted to the ABA's All-Rookie team, was hiding a dark secret. After home games, he'd head straight to his friendly pusher and purchase a supply of cocaine. In the privacy of his car, he'd get high before driving home. Today, Gerard, who has worked as a drug counselor for the past seventeen years, openly talks about how his all-consuming habit cost him his money, his family, and nearly his life. "Marvin and I went down similar paths for twenty years."

As a result of drug abuse, Gerard's stats nosedived after his first year in St. Louis. Over the course of his final six pro seasons, he averaged just 7.2 points and 2.4 rebounds. "My focus was on dope, not basketball."

In 1986, twelve years after Gerard's first hit and five years after he had retired from pro basketball, his wife discovered that the couple was $100,000 in debt. She confronted Gus, who broke down and confessed the humiliating details of his obsession with cocaine. Divorce papers were soon filed.

For a while, Gerard stayed at his mother's home in Union-town, Pennsylvania, where he financed his drug scores by earning $30 a night as a pizza delivery man. "I was so desperate and selfish that I started pilfering ten-dollar bills out of my mom's purse just so I could buy some pot. She never caught on to what I was doing or at least she never said anything to me, but I despised myself for stealing from her, so I decided to leave and move in with my brother's family." His visit, however, didn't last long before he was not-so-politely asked to find another place to live. "I spent my days walking around town, looking to mooch money from peo-ple I knew who felt sorry for me. Then I spent whatever cash I had scrounged up on dope," he says. "At night, I slept in my car or crashed at friends' homes."

What followed were years of fighting a losing battle against drug dependency and depression. Without any purpose in life, Gerard concluded he had no reason to live. Despite having earned $1.5 million during his career, he was now beyond broke, owing more than $26,000 in back child support for his son and daughter.

"There's no other way to put it: I was a deadbeat dad," he says. "Cocaine had meant more to me than taking care of my own children's needs, and I couldn't see any way I could ever make amends to them."

On May 25, 1993, a date that is forever etched in Gerard's mind, he made a fateful decision.

"For some reason, my thoughts turned to Bill Robinzine, a teammate of mine when I played for the Kansas City Kings," he says. "My mind raced back to the day in 1982 when I heard Bill had taken his own life. He had parked his car in his garage, left the engine running, and committed suicide by inhaling carbon monoxide. I remember thinking, 'That's a peaceful way to end your troubles.' I pictured him sitting in the quiet darkness, finally at rest, with no more demons to battle.

"I had nothing left to offer my children. Going out the same way Bill did was, in my mind, the reasonable thing to do."

So Gerard, who was staying at a friend's house in Madison, Ohio, managed to borrow $200 and bought some cocaine and two half-gallons of rotgut vodka. After making the purchases, he drove around town in his dinged-up 1977 Toyota Corolla. "My plan was that when I ran out of coke and booze, I was going to kill myself," he says. "I tried to convince myself that suicide was a chicken's way out, but deep down I felt that by taking my own life, I'd be getting out of everybody's way. If I could get up the nerve to end it all, I wouldn't be causing any more pain to all those I loved, and at the same time, my own pain would be over."

After a two-day binge, he snorted the last traces of coke and drove to his buddy's house, pulling his car into the garage and closing the door. Then he got back into his vehicle and passed out with the engine running. But the despondent former Spirit had overlooked one crucial detail while planning his demise: He had forgotten that the car's fuel tank was nearly empty.

"I don't know how long I had been out cold," he says, "but I woke up feeling groggy and sick to my stomach. I was just alert enough to realize why I was still alive: The car had run out of gas before I could breathe in enough fumes to get the job done. All I could do was laugh, probably at the fact that I had screwed up once again."

Stumbling into the house, Gerard walked to the kitchen and sat down at the breakfast table, attempting to clear his head. Scattered in front him was the Sunday edition of *The Cleveland Plain Dealer*. On the cover of *Parade* magazine was a picture of John Lucas, a friend from his playing days and a former cocaine abuser who had conquered his addiction and established a drug treatment facility in Houston. "I read the story of how he had turned his life around and phoned him right away," Gerard says. "After our talk, he wired me money for a bus ticket and I headed down to his rehab center the same day. I've been straight ever since."[1]

Freddie Lewis, a veteran All-Star point guard who had won three ABA championships as an Indiana Pacer, was the Spirits' voice of reason, the team captain, and Barnes's toughest critic. "Management wanted me to be Marvin's guardian angel," he says. "I was supposed to drive him to practice, make sure he didn't miss any team flights, and keep him focused on playing ball. In other words, I was the designated babysitter."

Barnes was scarcely in the market for those types of services.

In ESPN's 30 for 30 documentary *Free Spirits*, Barnes recalled a conversation he had when Lewis arrived in St. Louis. "I remember when [Lewis] came into the locker room, he pulled me aside and said, 'Marvin, I'm here to help you. I'm gonna make you a star—a superstar. And I'm here to watch you, to keep you out of trouble.'"

"I was the old man on the team," Lewis says. "My idea of fun was going home and relaxing in front of the boob tube at night. Marvin, he was a hell raiser, always looking to party. There was nothing I could do or say that was going to turn him into a saint. On the court, though, he was supremely gifted. If he'd been able to block out all the outside distractions, I swear he could have led the league in scoring and rebounding as a rookie."

---

1   Gerard eventually earned a degree in drug counseling, caught up on his support payments, and reunited with his children after eight years of separation.

Eleven

MARVIN VS. THE DOCTOR: A BRIEF SHINING MOMENT

Two hours before a St. Louis home game against the New York Nets in early March of 1975, Barnes was kicking back in his townhouse living room, snorting a few rails of cocaine with a high school friend from Providence. What the Spirits' leading scorer and rebounder didn't realize was that his homey had laced the white powder with PCP, a powerful hallucinogen commonly known in drug vernacular as "angel dust." By the time Bad News arrived at the arena, he was downright giddy and scatterbrained.

Meanwhile in New Jersey, the Silna brothers were hosting a party for fifty guests to watch the highly publicized televised matchup between Barnes and Julius Erving. From the opening tap, the Spirits' superstar-in-training was, to put it charitably, off his game. Laughing and chatting incessantly with opponents while leisurely trotting up and down the court, the supposed backbone of the St. Louis defense put up no resistance as the Nets rolled to a 124–96 win. On the offensive end, Barnes was equally useless, scoring a measly four points. The team owners, totally mortified, decided it was time to dish out a verbal spanking.

Two days later, the Silnas, along with Donald Schupak, the team's legal counsel, flew to St. Louis for a Spirits–Memphis Sounds game. Unaware that the Silnas were in the building, Barnes was unstoppable, scoring 54 points and pulling down 23 rebounds in a 122–114 overtime victory. As soon as the final buzzer sounded, he was told to report to the team's administration office, where he found the three executives staring coldly at him.

"Marvin, we watched the Nets game on TV the other night at my house," Ozzie Silna said in a calm but disgusted tone. "You were a disgrace. I've put my heart and soul, along with a substantial amount of my money, into putting this team together. I expect every one of my employees—the popcorn vendors, the ushers, the front office staff, and the players—to give me an honest day's work. You didn't do that against New York. I don't mind paying you a rather hefty salary, but you have to earn it. Otherwise, you're stealing from me, and I won't tolerate that."

Before Barnes could offer any sort of apology, the ownership group stormed out the door.

Despite an ugly 32–52 record, the Spirits qualified for the playoffs in their first season. The defending champion Nets, however, were waiting in the first round. Not only had New York finished 26 games ahead of St. Louis in the standings, but it had won all 11 regular-season meetings between the two teams, with the average margin of victory having been a whopping 16 points. Additionally, Erving had outscored Barnes by more than 11 points per game in their head-to-head battles. In fact, the Spirits' big gun had been held to eight points or less three times by the Nets defense.

"After our final regular-season game, I told everyone in the locker room that we could beat New York if we just played as a team and forgot about all the individual stats," Lewis says. "The only reaction I got was a bunch of guys snickering at me."

Members of the media strongly implied that Barnes was too respectful of Erving. *Newsday* reporter Doug Smith, for example, claimed the usually confident center/forward acted as if he were "clearly star struck" whenever he faced Dr. J & Co. The stinging criticism energized the rookie, who proceeded to put together a string of stellar performances that carried St. Louis to the greatest playoff series upset in ABA history.

The self-doubting Spirits managed to gain a split of the first two games at the Nassau Coliseum, the Nets' home court, as Barnes totaled 78 points and 30 rebounds. "I had never seen him so driven," said "Snapper" Jones, "but bottom line, we still had only beaten New York once in thirteen tries. To have a realistic chance of taking the series, we had to win the next two in our own building."

Despite facing constant double-teams, Barnes seared New York for 35 points and 14 rebounds in a 113–108 Game Three Spirits' victory at St. Louis Arena. "In my mind, that was the one we needed," says Lewis. "The way we played, I think it shot the Nets' confidence to hell. Everyone in our locker room was thinking, 'Hey, no joke, Freddie was right. We really can win this thing.'"

In Game Four, Barnes tallied 23 points, 20 rebounds, and three blocks, which offset Erving's 35 points, as the Spirits utilized their fastbreak to secure an 11-point victory. "Defensively, it was by far Marvin's best game of the year," said Spirits GM Harry Weltman. "The Nets couldn't get near the basket with him protecting the rim. After a while, they simply gave up and settled for nothing but outside jumpers."

Trailing three games to one, the Nets hoped to regroup on their home court. As expected, they ran every set play through Erving, who finished with 34 points. But the Spirits, who were down by nine with 1:53 left in regulation, staged a miraculous comeback to gain a 108–107 win, pulling off the series upset, 4–1. It was Lewis who led the furious last-ditch charge, harassing Erving into committing a backcourt violation and then hitting a jumper from the top of the key with three seconds left to cap a 29-point effort.

"In my 16-year pro career, I played in thirteen losing playoff series, and the one against St. Louis was probably the most heart-breaking," Erving would say shortly after he retired in 1987. "The Spirits were hungrier than us—and that shouldn't have been the case. We didn't show the right amount of anything: talent, desire, enthusiasm."

The Nets series proved to be not only the apex of Barnes's season but of his entire pro career. For the five games, he out-scored Erving, 153–137, outshot him 50 to 45 percent, and outrebounded him 78–49.

"It was one of the few times I ever saw anyone get the best of Julius," says Wally Rooney, who was a referee in the ABA and NBA for more than twenty-five years. "I officiated a couple of games in that series, and I could see Erving was becoming more and more frustrated. He was begging for calls and wasn't getting them. Barnes, on the other hand, was having the time of his life."

"Marvin was on a mission," says Hubie Brown. "He'd either drive right past everyone to the basket or pull up for an easy jumper in the lane. The Nets would sometimes put three guys on him, and it didn't matter at all."

It looked as if Barnes had become the dominating force every-one had been waiting to see. "He had proven he could outduel Erving," Weltman said years later. "His effort in that series gave us tremendous optimism for the future. Unfortunately, it turned out to be false hope."

The Spirits' chances for a second straight playoff series upset were all but snuffed out when Lewis suffered a season-ending ankle injury early in Game Three of the Eastern Division Finals against Kentucky. Without its veteran floor leader, St. Louis reverted to regular-season form, playing sloppy one-on-one basketball and falling to the Colonels in five games.

Having averaged 24 points and 15.6 rebounds for the year, Barnes beat out Denver forward Bobby Jones and Utah center Moses Malone for the ABA's Rookie of the Year honors.

"Statistically, Marvin had as good a season as almost anyone in the league," said Ozzie Silna years later. "Yes, he was inconsistent, but what rookie doesn't have his ups and downs? We chalked it up to inexperience and immaturity."

Two days after the season had ended, Barnes stopped over at Fly Williams's townhouse to smoke a joint. He was greeted at the front door by an out-of-work construction worker named Bruce Edwards, who was entertaining three attractive women in the living room.

After introducing himself to everyone, Barnes headed upstairs, passing two more stunning female guests who were sitting quietly on the flight of steps. Peeking into the master bedroom, he saw Williams intimately engaged with yet another beautiful admirer. Not wanting to disturb his teammate's concentration, he went back downstairs, again walking by the young ladies who were patiently waiting their turn to spend some quality time with Fly.

Reentering the living room, Bad News could no longer contain his curiosity.

"Hey, Bruce, where did all these fine young things come from?" he asked.

"Fly asked me to find him some nice-looking girls for the day," Edwards replied.

"You mean you know them all personally?" Barnes added incredulously.

"Sure do," Edwards said.

"Brother, you've got to start hanging with me."

And once Williams went home to Brooklyn for the summer, Barnes followed through on his suggestion, inviting Edwards to move into his three-bedroom townhouse in Chesterfield, Missouri. In return for free room and board, the appreciative guest made sure his host was never lacking for feminine companionship.

Barnes also took in Bruce's brother, Jimbo, who had recently been released from prison after serving seven years' hard time for assault. According to Bruce, his brother also had "a couple of murders under his belt." Ever attracted to society's criminal element, Bad News immediately formed a bond with the ex-con and hired him to be his bodyguard.

One afternoon Jimbo said to his new employer, "Got a guy I want you to meet. He practically runs St. Louis."

The pair then drove to the Norwood Court apartments, located in a quiet middle-class neighborhood, where Barnes, as instructed by Edwards, who remained in the car, rang the bell for Suite No. 4 from the lobby. A gruff voice crackled through a speaker box, asking the visitor to identify himself. "It's Marvin. Came here to meet you."

"Second floor. My door's unlocked. I'm buzzing you in."

Upon entering the residence, Barnes noticed that the living room was unfurnished, there were no ceiling lights, and the window drapes were tightly drawn. Walking down a dark hallway, he spotted a thin black man, probably around thirty-five years of age, sitting in the kitchen.

"C'mon in. Take a load off," said the sharply dressed stranger, who was wearing blue-tinted Ray-Ban sunglasses. "Everyone calls me Patch. Already know who you are. Got some coke on hand if you're interested. Real high-quality stuff."

The basketball star, not knowing a thing about the man's background except that he was some type of high mucky-muck around town, played it safe and took a pass. An interview then followed. For 20 minutes, Barnes fielded a series of questions, mostly personal in nature. As the conversation was about to end, Patch asked his visitor which women he was seeing on a regular basis. Despite the intrusive nature of the inquiry, the sociable playboy rattled off the names of three young ladies he was dating but hadn't slept with yet. "Come back here a week from today at 2 p.m.," the supposed heavy hitter said. "I'm going to throw a private little get-together for you."

That was Barnes's first encounter with Roosevelt Becton, *the* drug trafficking kingpin of America's heartland.

When the adventurous Spirit returned to the same apartment the following week, he was greeted warmly. "Welcome to my world," Patch shouted as the guest of honor walked in. With that, the three women Barnes had previously mentioned to his mysterious host paraded out of a bedroom, each one nude. The most attractive one was told to perform oral sex on Bad News and, before he could blink, she got down on her knees and did as she was ordered.

Such was the power commanded by Becton.

Twelve

THE ST. LOUIS CONNECTION

Prior to becoming involved in drug trafficking, Becton owned a popular St. Louis nightspot named the Fashion Palace, which was located at 71 Maryland Plaza in the upscale West End section of the city. Around the corner from the club were the Chase and the Park Plaza, both posh five-star hotels where US presidents, foreign dignitaries, Hollywood movie queens, and Frank Sinatra, along with his "Rat Pack," all stayed when they came to town.

"The Palace had a nice mix of customers—professional people, sports figures, politicians," Becton says. "It had a friendly atmosphere and was beautifully decorated. The place was always packed. Never any trouble. The problem I ran into was that certain folks around town, including the hotel owners, as well as the mayor and his City Hall cronies, were out to get me simply because we catered to a black crowd.

"My enemies kept trying to buy me out, but I wouldn't sell because business was booming. When they couldn't tempt me into making a deal, they took more drastic steps. First, they burned my nightclub to the ground. After I rebuilt it, they bombed the place. All that was left was the shell of the building and a pile of rubble. I knew they were never going to stop trying to destroy me, so I finally gave up and sold the property.

"At that point, I decided to become a marijuana distributor because some of the regulars at the Palace made their living by moving drugs. With all my connections, they thought I could be a major asset to them. Because all the people I knew who bought and sold weed were pulling in a fortune, I took a risk and started learning from them how to be a successful supplier."

Pot trafficking was indeed a burgeoning high-profit industry. President Richard M. Nixon's "War on Drugs" declaration in 1971 had proven to be nothing more than meaningless political rhetoric. Once regarded as merely a pastime of the "turn on and tune out" sixties hippie subculture, smoking weed was now rapidly gaining acceptance in all segments of the country's population. Tens of thousands of unappreciated, overwhelmed Vietnam vets were using marijuana to relieve the stress of feeling ostracized in their own homeland. On college campuses, passing a joint or two around at a Saturday night frat party was commonplace. Out in the sedate suburbs, smoking a little grass with neighborhood friends was becoming an enjoyable leisure time activity for young married couples. Even low-income working-class stiffs were able to get high as often as they desired because the drug was so inexpensive and easy to obtain.

Demand for cocaine, or "blow," as it was often called, was also on the rise.[1] Back in the seventies, the potent white powder, sometimes labeled the "Rich Man's Drug," was simplistically viewed as a fast-acting pick-me-up. Snorting a line or two during the middle of a frenzied workday was, in fact, becoming increasingly chic

---

1   In clinical terms, cocaine is an extremely powerful stimulant that triggers feelings of euphoria and increased energy. Its long-term adverse effects include strokes, heart attacks, bone damage, seizures, memory loss, and a decrease in learning ability.

among professionals in high-pressure positions such as corporate executives, movie stars, Wall Street traders, attorneys, politicians, and even medical personnel.

Having decided that becoming a cocaine wholesaler would involve too much risk, Becton took full advantage of the spiraling demand for weed, with buyers from across the country regularly traveling to St. Louis to negotiate multimillion-dollar deals with him. In return, the grateful gangster thanked his loyal clients by providing them with the most decadent form of entertainment— all-night orgies that featured an abundance of weed, coke, and booze.

Becton's illegal enterprise, which he operated out of his clothing store, B&E, on Martin Luther King Boulevard, flourished due to two principal factors: He was one of the few drug suppliers in the country who had access to almost unlimited quantities of "Grade A" marijuana, as he called it; and he was an astute businessman who knew how to avoid conflicts. "My organization was nothing like the one in *American Gangster*," he says, referring to the 2007 movie that starred Denzel Washington. "We were strictly non-violent. All the Hollywood films about cutthroat drug traffickers have shootouts in every scene. Well, I didn't even carry [a gun]. If I made a commitment to provide a specific amount of pot at an agreed-upon price, I personally made sure everything was delivered on time, as promised. My best customers were the Irish crime bosses and the Olivastro Italian mob in St. Louis. I needed them, and they needed me. Everyone involved was making a bundle of money. That's why we all got along peaceably."

In June of 1975, Barnes began to socialize frequently with Becton, hobnobbing his way into the mobster's inner circle in only a matter of weeks. As a strong bond was being formed between the happy-go-lucky jock and the cannabis czar of the Midwest, the trafficker began to disclose confidential details about his line of work, including the fact that his top two lieutenants, David

Finley and Nathaniel Yancy, were making between $75,000 and $100,000 a month—tax free, of course.

"When I found out what Patch's boys were making," Barnes said, "I started thinking to myself, 'Man, I'm in the wrong fucking business.' What really changed my life was when Patch took me into a spare room at his place. He had a million dollars scattered on a bed. As I stared at all that cash, he told me, 'I'm giving this to my wife, so she'll stop bitching and moaning about me not treating her with respect. I also have to take care of the other women in my life. They all live in nice pads and drive new cars. I just keep buying them gifts—a diamond necklace for one, a gold bracelet for another, and a Caribbean vacation for the third—to keep them all happy.'"

Naturally, the twenty-three-year-old racketeer wannabe was thoroughly impressed.

Barnes was soon offered the chance to earn big bucks the "easy way," by becoming a junior partner in the drug merchant's organization. His job description: orgy host. "All my buyers loved the guy, which, of course, was great for business," says Becton. "He was a natural PR man. When I'd take my clients to the Spirits games, we'd sit courtside and he'd come over and treat my guests as if he'd been their best friend for years.

"I didn't permit Marvin to sell pot, coke, or anything else. I didn't want to put him in a position of jeopardizing his career. I did my best to make sure playing basketball was his top priority because he had such a talent for the game. I let him make some good money on the side without having to do a damn thing because I wanted to bail him out of all his financial jams. There was absolutely nothing in it for me."

Once a month, Barnes was allowed to purchase 100 pounds of marijuana for $100 a pound. Becton would then personally resell it for him for a minimum price of $350 a pound. "I was basically giving Marvin a $25,000 gift every 30 days. At that time, I could afford to be generous because I was pulling in more money than I knew what to do with."

Barnes soaked it all up. The kid who had dreamed of being a mobster while growing up in Codding Court suddenly found himself living out his childhood fantasies—while being a professional basketball player at the same time.

Rumors, however, soon began to circulate that the syndicate's designated glad-hander was becoming a little too cozy with some truly dangerous people. "I found out that Marvin was experimenting with heroin," Becton says. "Back in those days, we called the stuff 'dog food.' He wasn't mainlining, mind you, but he was snorting up every now and then. He didn't have any idea that I was familiar with the lowlife pushers who were selling to him. I knew these pricks would just as soon put a bullet between his eyes than look at him. They couldn't have cared less that he played basketball for a living. If they thought he might talk too much or cross them, he was going to end up on a slab. I wanted him to stay away from all the dealers, and I told him so point blank."

Barnes wasn't any more savings conscious with his $300,000 annual supplementary income than he was with his basketball salary. He used some of his drug profits to pay down relatives' mortgages and helped out two members of his old Providence gang who were behind on their car loans. When Central High won another state title, he picked up the $1,400 tab for the players' leather championship jackets. There were also expensive items that he bought for himself—ornate watches and chains, four color TVs, top-of-the-line stereo equipment, a coyote fur jacket, and two pairs of alligator shoes. He also had thirteen phones installed in his townhouse—even though there were only eight rooms—plus the garage.

Neither credit cards nor checks were used to pay for his numerous transactions. "I didn't want the IRS snooping into my finances and asking me how I was getting my hands on all the money I was spending," Barnes said years later. "I dealt only in cold hard cash."

For months at a time, his Spirits paychecks lay atop his bedroom dresser as if the money he earned from playing basketball was nothing more than pocket change. "When I was working for Patch, I ran out of ideas for how to spend all the dough that was rolling in. I had so much cash in my townhouse that I kept $100,000 in twenty dollar bills underneath a mattress that one of my girlfriends slept on."

Barnes, it seemed, had found Utopia—that is, until Paul Edward Hindelang Jr., a former East St. Louis, Illinois, grade school teacher, entered the picture.

In the sinister world of drug running, Hindelang was a savant. Only twenty-four years old, he had formulated a nearly flawless scheme to smuggle marijuana into the US. Prior to coming to St. Louis, he had spent a year in Miami, somehow managing to cultivate a close friendship with Carlos Lehder, co-founder of Colombia's Medellin cartel. As a result of their mutual trust, the South American drug lord eventually agreed to supply "Big Ed," as his friends called him, with shipments of pot at a discounted wholesale price. The 6-foot blond entrepreneur then forged an alliance with Becton to distribute the weed throughout the country.

Hindelang had a mammoth ego, which was coupled with an insufferable personality. Barnes definitely was not a fan. "Ed was the only white guy in our organization, which made us all a little edgy when he first showed up. The guy treated everybody but Patch like he owned them because he was the one with all the international connections. He'd always brag about how he was going to make us all millionaires. I didn't want to hear that shit. Hell, I was already a millionaire—at least on paper.

"It wasn't until Patch took me aside and explained that Ed was for real that I started to put up with all his big talk. I had a good thing going and I didn't want this guy messing things up for me. So, even though I knew he thought of us as nothing but his personal slaves, I did the best I could to get along with him."

What set Hindelang apart from all other traffickers was his method of smuggling marijuana into the States. He pioneered and masterminded the concept of using a "mother ship," positioned in international waters three miles off Florida's Atlantic shoreline, as the base for his operations. The planning involved was meticulous and complex. According to one DEA official, the scheme was "pure genius."

Having such close ties to Lehder, all Hindelang had to do was make a single phone call to arrange for as much as 450,000 pounds of pot to be shipped from Colombia. He was even allowed to buy the grass on credit.

Once a delivery had begun, eight or nine large commercial fishing boats would rendezvous at different locations with the marijuana-filled mother ship as it steamed up Florida's east coast. At each transfer site, tightly packed bales of weed were loaded onto a trawler from the freighter before it continued its northward course.

After pulling away from the supply ship, the fishing vessels headed precisely one and a half miles toward shore where the illegal cargo was hoisted onto as many as forty "go-fast" speed boats and sailboats at varying times throughout the day. The pleasure crafts, which blended in with the Sunshine State's other 800,000 or so recreational boats, then fanned out while transporting the pot to secluded private docks in the Keys, Miami, Hollywood, Fort Lauderdale, Boca Raton, Pompano Beach, Palm Beach, and Fort Pierce.

Utilizing this elaborate relay system, the crews had little fear of being caught.

"We're not talking about moving a couple hundred pounds of marijuana," says one member of the Immigration and Customs Enforcement (ICE) operation that eventually was instrumental in bringing down what was believed to be the largest drug smuggling organization in the country. "Hindelang's underbosses had to hire huge men, mostly college and pro football players, to load and unload the pot because each bale weighed 120 pounds. Each transfer was completed in ten minutes or less. These traffickers were highly intelligent and efficient. Every move they made was planned down to the last detail."

After the boats docked, the pot was loaded onto waiting Winnebagos and 18-wheelers. Twelve drivers then delivered the product to buyers in Boston, New York, Philadelphia, Washington, Atlanta, Detroit, St. Louis, Dallas, New Orleans, Chicago, Phoenix, and Las Vegas.

Becton, Hindelang, and, on three occasions, Barnes, flew down to Fort Lauderdale on a private Lear jet to oversee both onshore and offshore logistics from a house they had rented for a week. "Everything always went smoothly," Becton says. "Most of the time we played cards and brought in some women to entertain us."

Big Ed never used his own funds to pay the approximately 120 men involved in a single smuggling operation. In fact, almost all of his money was safely invested through friends and relatives in real estate, business ventures, and foreign bank accounts. Instead, he would ask Becton to bankroll the hiring costs, which were roughly $3.5 million per shipment. In exchange for financing the undertaking, Becton was allowed to buy 180,000 pounds of marijuana for $110 a pound, which he then resold to his customers at a 300- to 400-percent profit. According to an ICE official,

Hindelang was paying the Colombians $100 a pound, which meant 100,000 pounds of marijuana cost him $10 million.

"After the weed had been delivered to the major buyers, Hindelang and his underlings would realize profits close to $35 million per shipment while Becton's organization would net approximately $20 million," said Chuck Visco, a sheriff from Monroe County, Florida, who years later investigated the crimes and the money trail.

Eventually, Hindelang, Barnes, Becton, and five trusted associates pooled their money to lease a freighter that had a 200-ton cargo hold. By using their own ship to pick up the marijuana at the Colombian port of Santa Marta and deliver it off the coast of Florida, the drug runners were able to increase their profits by approximately 15 percent since Lehder, not having to pay for shipping costs, was willing to sell the high-grade grass to Big Ed & Co. for the discounted price of $75 per pound.

Because Hindelang was generously supplying Becton's top aides with complimentary drugs, Barnes was now more than willing to forgive his arrogance. "Ed started taking good care of me, and I actually started to like how he did business," he admitted. "The man was sharp and totally ruthless. Nobody could take that away from him."

The more money Becton accumulated, the more bighearted he became in providing Barnes with financial security. Gradually the Spirits' headliner grew to be so immersed in the trafficker's lifestyle that he regarded basketball as nothing more than a casual hobby.

Thirteen

HIGH ON COCAINE

Six days before the start of the ABA's 1975–76 season, the Baltimore Claws, formerly the Memphis Sounds, folded. Eleven games into the schedule, the San Diego Sails ceased operations. A week and a half later, the Utah Stars declared bankruptcy. With only seven teams remaining, the shrinking league was on its last leg.

Spirits coach Bob MacKinnon had moved on to become player personnel director of the Buffalo Braves in the NBA. Thirty-four-year-old Rod Thorn, who had been an assistant with the Nets, was named as his replacement. One of the new coach's first moves was to cut Barnes's coke-snorting comrade, Fly Williams. "Above average individual scorer, but he couldn't grasp the concept of team basketball," says Thorn. "Let me put it this way: When a guy flat out refuses to pass the ball on a three-on-one break, it's time to send him packing."

Williams, who stayed in St. Louis for a few months following his release and occasionally partied with and supplied drugs to his ex-teammates when they were on the road, would spend the rest of his career playing in the minor leagues and overseas before returning to the streets of New York City, where obtaining cocaine became his sole obsession. In 1987, an hour after playing pick-up in his Brownsville neighborhood, he was shot in the back while attempting a robbery. The gun blast blew apart one of his lungs, a kidney, and a third of his stomach. "All I remember," Fly stated in his autobiography, *The Fly 35*, "is watching blood filling up in my shoes. It was a miracle I didn't end up dead." For his crime, the schoolyard legend served fourteen months in prison.

Thorn understood the necessity of establishing a solid working relationship with the team's top gate attraction. "Shortly before our opening game, I sat down with Marvin for an hour," the former Spirits coach remembers. "I stressed that I needed him to be the team leader, on and off the court. He said all the right things, and I left that meeting thinking the two of us were on the same page. The very next day he blew off practice. I mean, where do you go from there?"

Barnes made no effort to conceal the fact that he was running with a shady crowd. "He was constantly surrounded by loudmouth types who always looked like they were itching for trouble," says Thorn. "I repeatedly warned him not to invite problems. I told him to get rid of all the hangers-on. He made all sorts of promises to me, but his behavior never changed. It was extremely frustrating because here was a guy whose natural abilities made you want to believe he was on the verge of greatness.

"The guy was one of the most exceptional players I've ever seen, but I can't honestly say he was Hall of Fame material because the truly elite competitors share one trait he didn't possess. They're always dependable, willing to do whatever it takes to win. Marvin couldn't or wouldn't commit to playing at such a high level every time he put on the uniform."

In December of '75, Becton ordered all members of his organization who were single to get married. At first, Barnes thought the edict had to be some kind of joke, but his boss clearly was not in the kidding mood. "I'm dead serious," Patch told Barnes. "You have to tone things down and start blending in. You think people don't notice when a dozen cars pull up to your place at two in the morning? Your neighbors have eyes and ears, and they're not idiots. They see all the people staggering in and out, drunk out their minds or high on drugs. They hear all the noise. This shit has to end before the cops figure out what's going on and take down my entire operation."

Obeying Becton's command, Barnes, after a one-week "engagement," wed a woman named Barbara, whom he had known for only a few months. "She was a very nice lady, but the marriage was a total sham. We got an annulment less than a year later. No hard feelings either way."

Midway through the season, it became apparent that Barnes and Lucas could no longer peacefully coexist in St. Louis. "They were always at each other's throats. The tension was palpable. One of them had to go," said Harry Weltman. "We needed a center and [Kentucky's] Caldwell Jones was available. Reluctantly, I traded Maurice, mainly because the Colonels had major reservations about Marvin's work ethic and his off-the-court conduct."

One particular game between St. Louis and Kentucky following the trade is seared into the memory of former Spirit M. L. Carr. "It was a home game for us, and Lucas and Barnes were matched up at power forward. Maurice was getting killed so bad that the Colonels had to put their center, Artis Gilmore, on Marvin to try keeping him away from the basket. That didn't work either because Marvin ended up with 49 points and 31 rebounds. I didn't witness another performance like that until 1985 when Larry Bird scored 60 against the Atlanta Hawks in New Orleans."

Despite his increasing dependency on dope, Barnes was selected to play in the ABA All-Star Game for a second time. "His averages were solid, right around 25 [points] and 16 [rebounds] at the break," said Weltman, "but he was the most up-and-down player I ever saw. He'd score 50 one game and five the next. There were far too many nights when he was invisible on the court."

St. Louis guard Mike Barr, in particular, was openly critical of Barnes's erratic production. "It's obvious that basketball isn't Number One in Marvin's heart," he told *St. Louis Post-Dispatch* reporter Rick Hummel, "but I don't know what is."

Responding to the growing number of disparaging comments, Bad News went on the offensive. "I'm a basketball player, not a monk. I play the women, I play the clothes, I play the cars. There are players, and there are playees," he told the media. "The players are the ones who play the playees. I'm a player." Then, after pausing a few seconds for effect, he smiled and said, "To know me is to love me, and you don't know anybody who doesn't love News, do you?"

It was the flamboyant Spirit's quirky personality that helped deflect questions about whether he was a drug user. "I don't think anyone quite figured out what made him tick," Carr says. "At times he was on another planet. Honestly, he seemed to enjoy being thought of as just plain nuts."

"During my time playing for the Spirits, I never had an inkling that Marvin had a substance abuse problem," veteran NBA coach and former Spirits teammate Mike D'Antoni says. "It just goes to show that enormous talent can mask almost anything. If someone had told me that he was a cokehead, I would have thought the idea was laughable. Everybody could see he marched to the beat of his own drum. But him being a druggie? That never crossed my mind."

An infatuation with the lifestyle of hardened criminals led to Barnes carrying two guns at all times. "I always kept a roll of cash, sometimes two or three grand, in my right front pants pocket," he explained later, "and I also had enemies on the streets who were threatening to kill me. Had to protect myself. When someone asked me why I needed two guns, I'd tell them, 'If one misfires, I always have the other one to get the job done.'"

Ultimately, Becton became irritated by his minor partner's stone-cold killer act. "I told him to concentrate on basketball or I was through with him. I let him know that I'd tell everyone who did business with me that he was too unstable to trust. I sat him down and said, 'Marvin, you'll have a target on your back if you don't listen carefully to me. Got it?'"

Barnes didn't get it. Before one home game, he got high and burst into the St. Louis locker room waving around what turned out to be an unloaded pistol. "I'm going to kill every last one of you bitches," he yelled at his teammates. "You all ain't nothing but a bunch of backstabbers."

Guard Don Chaney was the first to dive for cover, hiding under the trainer's table. "I wasn't sure if News was serious or not, but I wasn't taking any chances. With him, you never knew. Luckily, it was just his idea of a prank."

In late January, with St. Louis's record at 20–27, Thorn was fired. The Silna brothers and Weltman cited Thorn's inability to "effectively communicate" with Barnes as one of the primary reasons for his dismissal. Highly respected former Providence coach Joe Mullaney, who also had an impressive pro resume, was brought in to take over the bench duties. He had guided the Friars to 318 wins from 1955 until 1969, and management's thinking was that he could bring a sense of stability to Marvin's wildly immature life. The strategy proved to be a monumental failure.

After a month of Barnes's unexcused absences from practices, missed flights, and late arrivals to games, Mullaney demanded that the team heavily fine its man-child. When the exasperated coach was informed that the Spirits' undependable star still owed more than $24,000 for past rules violations, he snapped, "Well, then suspend him without pay."

"If we did that," a panicky club executive told Mullaney, "he might just pick up and leave town altogether. Then what would we do?"

The veteran coach couldn't fathom management's logic, or rather its lack thereof. "They thought the future of the franchise rested on the shoulders of Marvin Barnes," Mullaney would later tell Pluto. "To me, that was a frightening thought."

Barnes was not enamored with his new coach. "MacKinnon was real cool, a man who knew the game inside out. Thorn was the hyper type, always pacing, flapping his arms and jumping up and down on the sideline. I called him "Big Bird." He took some getting used to, but I could handle him. But I don't know about this Mullaney character. He's a screamer," the outspoken Spirit complained to Hummel. "He's yelling five different things at me—run, shoot, rebound, pass, get back on defense. Damn, I can't do them all at once."

Barnes's opinionated views went far beyond his own situation. Rookie M. L. Carr once made the mistake of seeking out his more established teammate for career advice. Late in the regular season, the 6-foot-5 swingman had been asked by Weltman if he would be interested in signing an extension. The twenty-four-year-old most assuredly could have used the security of a guaranteed multi-year deal since he had been previously cut by Kentucky of the ABA and also by Kansas City and Boston of the NBA.

"I mentioned to Marvin that the Spirits wanted to renegotiate my contract. He told me to ask for a three-year deal for $400,000, with at least $100,000 of it being paid as a signing bonus. As soon as I told Weltman that I wanted six figures up front, the

A wide-open Marvin Barnes (No. 24) nails a 15-foot jumper in a 101–65 Providence victory over St. Francis College of New York on February 16, 1974, at the Civic Center.

As Austin Peay defenders Percy Howard (23) and Fly Williams (35) move in too late, Barnes knocks down a clutch basket that helped Providence gain a 94–92 win on December 15, 1973. For the game, the Friar center set team records for most field goals (23) and most points (52). He also totaled 19 rebounds.

Barnes boxes out an Austin Peay defender and scores on a rebound tip-in.

Soaring above an opponent, Barnes blocks a layup attempt by swatting the ball off the backboard.

Photos courtesy of Thomas F. Maguire Jr.

As Barnes and an opponent square off, Spirits teammate Maurice Lucas steps in before any punches could be exchanged. Barnes usually wasn't the one to start a fight, but would be the first to stand up for a teammate.

Watching intently from the Spirits bench are (from left) guard Mike Barr, Barnes, forward Eugene "Goo" Kennedy, and guard Steve "Snapper" Jones.

Julius Erving, a.k.a. "Dr. J," displays perfect form as he releases a pull-up jumper over Barnes and Spirits captain Freddie Lewis.

Driving down the lane, Barnes releases a running hook shot over Nets forward Julius Erving (32) while St. Louis power forward Maurice Lucas (20) positions himself near the basket for a possible rebound.

Always a showman, Barnes throws down an
emphatic slam.

Barnes, who wore "Marvin" on the back of his jersey,
stretches prior to tipoff.

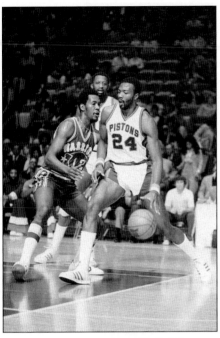

Detroit head coach Herb Brown restrains Barnes after the forward was shoved from behind while attempting a dunk.

Golden State Warriors forward E. C. Coleman (12) seals off the lane as power forward Barnes, now with the Detroit Pistons, looks for an opening.

Barnes (8), playing for the Buffalo Braves, banks in a short jumper as Houston Rockets defenders Kevin Kunnert (44) and John Lucas (15) are both caught flatfooted.

Portland Trail Blazer Maurice Lucas attempts to squeeze past a Celtics tandem of Barnes (27) and guard Chris Ford (42).

Photos courtesy of AP Images

A smiling youngster looks on as Barnes signs an autograph for him following
a Spirits win at the St. Louis Arena.

Legends (from left to right) Connie Hawkins, Marvin Barnes, Julius Erving, Charlie Scott, and George Gervin pose for a
picture at the ABA's 30th anniversary banquet on August 23, 1997.

conversation ended. Next game I was taken out of the starting lineup. Marvin felt terrible because his advice had backfired on me, so he faked a back injury early in the first quarter just to get me extra playing time. Afterwards, he went out of his way to tell the media that the team should give me an extension because I was such a 'valuable asset.' I guess management wasn't paying attention to what he said because I never got another offer."

Fortunately for Carr, he did receive a three-year $500,000 free-agent contract from the Detroit Pistons in the offseason and went on to enjoy a ten-year NBA career that included two championship seasons with the Boston Celtics. "In a roundabout way, I guess I should thank Marvin for that. But at the time he tried to help me out with St. Louis, I thought he just might have ruined my whole future."

On paper, the Spirits appeared to be one of the favorites to win the 1976 ABA Championship. The talent-laden roster, led by Barnes, also featured Mike D'Antoni, Ron Boone, Caldwell Jones, Don Chaney, M. L. Carr, Freddie Lewis, and twenty-one-year-old Moses Malone, whose contract had been bought from the financially strapped Utah Stars a month into the season.[1]

Nevertheless, the team turned out to be a dud, finishing out of the playoffs in sixth place at 35–49, ahead of only the Virginia Squires, who'd won just 19 games and then folded days after the end of the regular season. Over the course of the final five weeks of play, during which time the Spirits went 2–10, Barnes's production

---

1   The 6-foot-10 Malone, a board-crashing brute, would go on to win three MVP awards and five rebounding titles in the NBA.

Fourteen

MOTOWN MADNESS

Details of the NBA's leveraged takeover of the ABA in May 1976 came as no surprise. With the merger, the ABA's Spirits of St. Louis and Kentucky Colonels had been left for dead.

"The NBA only wanted to add four teams: the Spurs, Nuggets, Nets, and Pacers," former Spirits GM Weltman said. "They were adamant about it. What hurt our franchise the most was that home attendance was so miserable [an 'announced' 3,728 fans per game]. Still, I can't help but wonder if things might have turned out differently had Marvin lived up to his potential. But because our marquee player was so inconsistent, so disruptive, we were viewed as a shaky organization almost from the beginning."

The defunct Spirits did, however, become the most profitable team never to play in the NBA, thanks to Ozzie Silna, who negotiated the shrewdest business deal in pro sports history.

In order for the merger to take place, all six ABA franchises, including the two that were being dissolved, had to approve the financial terms. Kentucky owner John Y. Brown, having secured a deal to purchase the Buffalo Braves in the NBA for $6.2 million, agreed to fold the Colonels in return for $3.3 million. Silna, however, held out. Threatening to derail the entire process of forming a single, 22-team pro league, the St. Louis owner insisted on an equitable long-term settlement. In exchange for killing off the Spirits, he demanded $2.2 million in cash and a 14.7-percent share of the four assimilated ABA teams' television revenues *in perpetuity*, a phrase that haunts NBA executives to this day. Because league income from game telecasts at the time was next to nothing, the proposal was accepted with little debate.

Acceding to Silna's terms turned out to be an epic miscalculation on the part of the NBA. As the league's popularity exploded in the eighties and nineties, TV rights were sold to CBS and then NBC for staggering sums of money. Additional megabuck deals were later negotiated with TNT, ESPN, ABC, and TBS. As a result, NBA television revenues soared into the hundreds of millions of dollars annually, thus enabling St. Louis ownership to become filthy rich.

The Silna brothers each took a 45-percent cut of the St. Louis settlement while the team's legal counsel, Donald Schupak, was given the remaining 10-percent share by the franchise's owners. Over the next thirty-eight years, the three beneficiaries of the pact collected an estimated total of $325 million from the league. Despite numerous attempts to discover a legal loophole, the NBA was never able to force a modification of the 1976 agreement.[1]

A few weeks after the merger with the ABA had been ratified, the NBA held a dispersal draft to determine which teams would

---

1   In January of 2014, the league announced that a settlement of $500 million had been reached to terminate the "in perpetuity" TV revenue payments to the Spirits owners. Under the terms of the revised agreement, the Silna partnership would now receive an undisclosed annual percentage of revenue from NBA-TV, foreign TV rights, and On-Demand League Pass from the four former ABA clubs that were assimilated into the NBA when the leagues merged in '76. The teams, however, do have the right to end the revenue royalty payments by negotiating a final buyout with the St. Louis group at a future date.

acquire the contracts of players on the Spirits' and Colonels' rosters. A fee for the rights to each individual was established, with clubs choosing in inverse order of their 1975–76 records.

The first to be selected was 7-foot-2 Artis Gilmore, who went to the Chicago Bulls for a rights fee of $1.1 million. Maurice Lucas was then taken by the Portland Trail Blazers, who paid a mere $300,000 to purchase his contract. After Ron Boone was picked third by the Kansas City Kings, who shelled out $250,000, Barnes, with a steep price tag of $500,000, was scooped up by the Detroit Pistons. Moses Malone was the fifth player chosen, going to the Trail Blazers for a piddling $350,000. He was subsequently traded to the Buffalo Braves for a '78 first-round draft pick.

A total of twelve players from the two defunct ABA clubs were drafted. Those not taken became free agents.

Several teams that could have bought the rights to Barnes's long-term contract concluded that acquiring the former ABA Rookie of the Year would be too much of a gamble. "No one doubted his immense talent, but you'd hear numerous stories about him being a constant distraction, a bad influence," said Dr. Jack Ramsay, who had been named head coach of the Trail Blazers several weeks before the dispersal draft was held. "I think his reputation scared away some people, including us."

From all indications, though, Bad News was most welcome in Motown. The Pistons, coming off a lackluster 36–46 season, had been seeking a workhorse power forward to team with All-Star center Bob Lanier underneath the basket. It seemed like the ideal situation.

Except in the muddled mind of Marvin.

The rigors of being an addict/athlete had taken their toll. At the ripe old age of twenty-four, Barnes felt completely burnt out. Since the end of the Spirits' season in April, he had spent all his time snorting coke, smoking weed, and hosting orgies. Between his extensive drug use and crowded late-night social schedule, he couldn't find time to squeeze in even an occasional light workout.

"I could never admit it at the time, but I was this close to being a junkie," he said, holding his thumb and forefinger a fraction of an inch apart. "I had always considered myself a star, a celebrity, and I enjoyed looking the part. But after the Spirits folded, all I cared about was getting high."

Once a snappy, meticulously neat dresser, he now was frequently spotted around downtown St. Louis wearing T-shirts, baggy sweat pants, and cruddy sneakers that had no shoelaces. He seldom shaved, often settled for "Right Guard showers" instead of taking the time to use soap and water, ate nothing but fast food, and got little to no sleep. His weight dropped 25 pounds in three months.

In Barnes's opinion, it didn't make sense to continue playing basketball. Mentally drained, the former king of the crazies formulated a radical strategy: He would take a year's sabbatical, relax for a while, and gradually work himself back into shape. Once rejuvenated, he'd make a spectacular comeback with the Pistons. An integral part of his master plan was that while on hiatus, he would continue to work for Becton in order to maintain a positive cash flow.

The notion of him taking a career detour did not meet with the trafficker's approval. "If you quit playing ball," Patch told Barnes, "you're out of my organization for good."

The rebuke left the mobster's protégé with no alternative but to join the Pistons, but before Bad News would agree to report, he informed the media that his contract would have to be renegotiated. When Detroit General Manager Oscar Feldman shot down the bold demand, the renegade forward felt slighted. "Marvin Barnes doesn't beg," he declared, referring to himself in the third person. So, sans representation, he decided to hold out.

"Friends of mine in the ABA had forewarned me that the guy could be selfish and unreliable," says Feldman. "After he refused to show up on time for training camp, I was livid. We had just paid $500,000 for his rights, and before he had even arrived in Detroit he was complaining to the media about being underpaid and underappreciated."

After two weeks of fruitless telephone discussions, an in-person meeting was arranged. Barnes's bluff was about to be called.

"You know I'm not going to cave in," Feldman told him. "Show me that you can play at a consistently high level and I'll think about restructuring your deal. Make me a believer. Become an All-Star in this league. Then we'll talk. Right now, all you're doing is wasting my time."

The disconsolate malcontent conceded defeat and joined the team. When asked by a reporter if he envisioned being a starter, Barnes, smug as ever, answered, "Damn straight, cuz. News didn't come here to sit on no wood."

Off the court, Marvin's life had taken a turn for the better. He and Debbe Santos, whom he had dated regularly since his freshman year in college, had become the proud parents of a beautiful baby girl named Tiffani. But even the blessed event wasn't a lifestyle changer for the self-absorbed Pistons power forward, who still preferred to score cocaine rather than score points.

The Motor City definitely was not an ideal environment for someone with Barnes's mindset. Drug use in the city was rampant. Violent crime had turned the metropolitan area into a 1,337-square-mile blood-soaked battleground. The economy had yet to recover from the effects of Detroit's 1967 race riots, which left 43 dead, 1,189 injured, 7,200 arrested, and more than 2,000 buildings and homes destroyed by fires. According to Michigan statistics, the local unemployment rate in 1976 was 21 percent, nearly three times the US average.

The atmosphere inside the locker room was a reflection of the city's turbulent times. "Almost everyone on the team carried a licensed firearm," Barnes said. "There were so many guys who owned a piece that we started calling ourselves the 'Detroit Hoodlums.'"

According to Pistons teammate M. L. Carr, there was one detail Bad News might have gotten wrong concerning the players' private gun collection. "I'm not so sure about the 'licensed' part. In Detroit, you could buy a pistol on almost any street corner. I guarantee they didn't come with no licenses."

Thirty minutes into his first preseason practice, Barnes went up for a rebound and landed awkwardly. Feeling a burning sensation down his right leg, he limped off the court. In the locker room, the team doctor ordered X-rays, which came back negative. Media members insinuated the new arrival had faked the injury because he simply did not have the stamina to get through a full workout.

"Reporters were dogging me, telling the world I was a head case."

Becton, suspecting that his friend was being set up, arranged for a second opinion. On October 9, 1976, Barnes arrived at Detroit's Metro Airport to catch a flight to Ann Arbor, where he was scheduled to be examined by an orthopedic specialist at the University of Michigan Hospital. At the ticket counter, he attempted to check a gym bag that contained an unloaded .38 Special, but was told it was too late to load any baggage onto the plane. Rather than store the gun in an airport locker, the

Pistons forward proceeded directly to the boarding gate. At the security checkpoint, he placed the carryall on a conveyer belt for inspection. As soon as it went through the X-ray machine, horns and sirens blared from all directions. Five officers, weapons drawn, surrounded Barnes, who was promptly handcuffed and led away. Later that day, he was bailed out by Carr and released on his own recognizance. Because the firearm was empty, only a misdemeanor charge was filed.

Back in Providence, an alert police detective read about the arrest and ascertained there were still two weeks remaining on Barnes's three-year probation term that he had received in 1973 for the Ketvirtis assault. And so, a warrant was issued for him to appear in Rhode Island Superior Court for violating the terms of his parole. He was subsequently sentenced to one year in state prison by Judge Anthony Giannini, who ruled that Pistons forward could finish the basketball season before reporting to the Adult Correctional Institution in Cranston.

Days after having resumed practicing, Barnes complained to Head Coach Herb Brown that he was still in excruciating pain. Although few in the front office believed the claim, Brown told Feldman that it was obvious the power forward's injury had not fully healed.

When the throbbing ache in Barnes's leg intensified, a new set of X-rays was taken, which revealed he had suffered a broken fibula. Although the team physician was forced to admit there was a fracture, he told the media that the injury "is the kind that some guys have played with. It's a hairline break, that's all." The reserve power forward was placed on injured reserve and sat out the first 17 games of the season.

"That doctor did a great job of covering his own ass," Barnes said years later. "Here I had been practicing on a broken leg and this quack made it sound like it was no big deal."

Once reactivated, Barnes, still determined to renegotiate his contract, decided to pad his stats by shooting the ball almost every time he touched it. The media, along with some teammates, questioned his often times absurd shot selection. "Got to get my 20 [points] a night," Marvin said. "The fans be demanding it."

The 1976–77 Pistons drew an average crowd of only 5,448, which ranked 20th out of the NBA's 22 teams. The club's most loyal supporters, according to Barnes, were hookers, pimps, dope dealers, and drunks. "They all loved me because their life-style mirrored mine. I'd always make sure my East Side gangster friends had prime seats right behind our bench. After the games, win or lose, I'd walk out to my car and throw a party right in the parking lot. Everybody was welcome. We had booze, reefer, and plenty of the high-test stuff. Guys from the Tigers, Red Wings, and Lions were always stopping by. [Four Tops lead singer] Levi Stubbs, a poker buddy of mine, Marvin Gaye, and [Temptations lead vocalist] David Ruffin showed up once in a while when they weren't on tour. All the tailgating made me a ghetto legend."

Of course, rumors were always swirling concerning Barnes's penchant for drugs. "I'd be lying if I said I didn't hear any stories," Herb Brown admits. "There was one time in Los Angeles when the management at our hotel alerted the DEA that Marvin and a couple other players were smoking pot and using cocaine. A bellman supposedly tipped off the guys before the agents could organize a raid. There was other gossip going around about Marvin, but I ignored it all because I thought the world of the guy. His teammates felt the same about him. As far as I was concerned, he was an awesome person who genuinely cared about people, especially children. He'd sneak a group of inner city kids into nearly every game. Afterwards, he gave every one of them enough money to buy a new pair of sneakers or a basketball and treated them to ice cream. I called him the Pied Piper because a bunch of underprivileged kids were always following him around. I'll never say a bad word about him, and my brother Larry feels exactly the same way as I do."

Barnes sustained his second major injury of the season in late March when Houston forward Dwight Jones hacked him on the right hand, fracturing the fourth metacarpal as he attempted a layup. "I wasn't hit that hard," he would say years later, "but all my coke snorting had turned my bones into twigs."

The Pistons finished the regular season at a respectable 44–38, earning home court advantage against the Golden State Warriors in the preliminary round of the playoffs. Ruled out for the post-season due to his broken finger, Barnes wanted to begin serving his prison sentence immediately. Therefore, he announced to the press that he would not be with the team during the playoffs because "there's nothing in my contract which obligates me to show up."

In response, management issued a terse press release that termed the pronouncement "absurd and selfish." Feldman met with the disgruntled forward, who had averaged a disappointing 9.6 points during his first NBA season, and threatened to fine him $25,000 and suspend him indefinitely if he were to walk out on the team. Grudgingly, Barnes cancelled his travel plans and, dressed in what he called his "Super Fly" outfits, sat stone-faced at the end of the bench as Detroit fell to Golden State, 2–1, in the best-of-three series.

Because Rhode Island authorities had ruled that Barnes did not have to report to prison until ten days after the Pistons' final game, he, along with Debbe, hopped a plane to Las Vegas for a pre-incarceration fling hours after Detroit had been eliminated. "We had one hell of a time," said Barnes. "I even won $10,000 playing blackjack. I used most of my profits to celebrate a little, if you get my drift."

From Sin City, the couple caught a flight to Providence, where they were picked up by a limousine and driven to a hotel where Becton and Hindelang, who had flown in from St. Louis by private jet, were waiting to give their pal a proper sendoff before he headed off to prison.

Two minutes before the midnight deadline to turn himself in, Bad News, mugging for TV cameras, strolled into the Adult Correctional Institution.

ACI was one of the roughest penitentiaries in the country. Rapes, stabbings, and savage brawls were everyday occurrences, with murderers, street thugs, mafia bosses, drug dealers, and sex offenders all sharing the same cellblocks.

In many ways, though, being incarcerated at that particular prison was like a homecoming for Barnes, who was a friend of a number of convicts locked up there. In fact, he was assigned the cell next to his former bodyguard from St. Louis, Jimbo Edwards. Marvin had invited him to Providence during the summer of 1976 and, while in town, Edwards, along with a girlfriend, had been nabbed attempting to rob a bank. Another prisoner, Gerry Ouimette, who called the shots for the Providence mob from behind bars after having been convicted of conspiring to commit murder, was a longtime acquaintance. Also providing company for the basketball star at the dilapidated ninety-nine-year-old facility was his brother-in-law, Dougie Gomes, who was serving time for assault and battery.

Barnes had previously visited ACI following his rookie season with the Spirits. At that time, the young pro who seemed destined for greatness was treated like royalty as he toured the complex and played one-on-one against some of the inmates. Before leaving, he deposited $50 into each prisoner's commissary spending account. "So when I got sent up there, I was cool with the brothers, the whites, and the Hispanics. I ran things in that place.

We had a black activist club, the African American Society, which I set up with the warden's permission. Naturally, I was top dog. The organization was given its own private phone, and I got to pick a personal assistant to answer any calls that came in for me."

He also smooth talked the warden into allowing each inmate to receive one visit per week in the prison library from civic-minded individuals in the Providence metropolitan area. It just so happened that the upstanding "community leaders" who showed up were always the girlfriends or wives of the prisoners. Soon the library's reference room became ACI's not-so-secret love nest.

Two months prior to his October parole date, Barnes was transferred from the maximum to medium security building, which inmates referred to as the "Cranston Country Club."

In the less restrictive environment, inmates lived in "cells" that were actually comfortable, decent-sized rooms (for prison standards, that is). For Barnes, it was almost like being back in a Providence dorm. He had an 18-inch color TV, a mahogany bureau, a nine-foot long bed, and plenty of privacy. A friend, Stevie Robinson, who was serving a six-year sentence, had such luxuries as a reclining leather chair and a house phone with an outside line, which he regularly used to order late-night deliveries from a nearby sandwich shop.

Once Barnes settled in, he paid two guards $300 apiece each week to look the other way while his girlfriends, all smuggling in drugs, showed up one by one at the visitors' room to chat and bring him their discreetly wrapped care packages. The bribe money was courtesy of Patch, who was still sending Bad News his standard cut of the marijuana trafficking operation's profits.

"This is fact," Barnes said, "I was selling the best cocaine and weed in all of New England right out of my cell."

When the celebrity felon wasn't peddling coke inside prison walls, he was snorting it, line after line—right in front of the grateful jailers who were receiving their generous under-the-table weekly stipends. "There were so many different kinds of drugs being passed around that I was always experimenting with something new and different."

If ever there were a perfect case of inmates running the asylum, ACI would have been it. But could all of Marvin's stories about "the good life" behind bars possibly be true? Absolutely, says former State Police Superintendent Brenden Doherty: "Back in the seventies, ACI was one of the most corrupt prisons in the country. When state investigators finally looked into all the crooked dealings taking place there, they cleaned house, top to bottom. As for the guards who were on the take, they were not only fired, but several were arrested and eventually found guilty of accepting bribes."

While Barnes was serving his time, Providence College helped him get closer to earning his bachelor's degree. Twice a week, the school sent Father Robert Morris and Professor Matthew Smith to teach private, one-hour classes in English literature and history. After receiving 'B' grades in both courses, Barnes attributed his academic success at ACI to one factor: "I couldn't cut classes," he told *Providence Journal* columnist Bill Reynolds, "because there was no place for me to go."

On Bad News's final night in prison, his fellow inmates presented him with a special parting gift—five grams of saran-wrapped high-quality cocaine, which he stuffed into one of his back pants pockets.

Waiting outside the steel doors of ACI when Barnes emerged at midnight was a chauffeured Rolls Royce owned by a well-known Rhode Island attorney, Raul Lovett, who had represented him in several civil court matters. Also on hand were Lanier, Brown, and Feldman, who had become the Detroit Pistons' team counsel and a minority owner of the club. Barnes was driven home to spend a few hours with Lula and then taken to T. F. Green International Airport in Warwick, Rhode Island. From there, the Detroit contingent caught an 8:30 a.m. flight to Buffalo, where the team was scheduled to play an exhibition game against the Braves at 1 p.m.

At a Memorial Auditorium press conference, the sleep-deprived parolee appeared uncharacteristically fidgety as he fielded questions about his playing shape, attitude, and prison experiences. "I was sweating bullets, not because the reporters were grilling me or anything like that, but because I still had the five grams of coke in my pocket. I was scared to death it would slip out and fall on the floor while I was talking to the media."

Once the interview ended, Barnes scurried into the locker room, discreetly stashed his "valuables," and changed into his uniform. It was back to business as usual for the "rehabilitated" ex-con.

For the first three weeks of the 1977–78 season, the rogue forward stayed at the home of Herb Brown, who had always been in his corner. With the coach's encouragement, Barnes produced respectable stats, averaging 11.5 points and 7.8 rebounds during the month of November. But when rumors started to swirl that the Pistons were about to fire Brown, Bad News rebelled.

Hoping to force a trade, the disenchanted veteran again asked Feldman for a raise. "You're shooting about 43 percent, and you honestly think I should reward you for that?" the Pistons GM said. "Come on, you have to do a lot better before I could even think of restructuring your contract. Right now you're making $300,000 a year. And to be perfectly honest, that's more than you deserve."

"If that's what you think, then get me the fuck out of here," Barnes replied.

There were credible rumors going around the league that the Knicks were in the market for a power forward who was a force on the boards. New York's All-Star center Bob McAdoo was averaging 14 rebounds a game, but their next-leading inside player, Lonnie Shelton, was averaging only six and a half. Barnes figured he'd be taking up residence in the Big Apple within a matter of days. The trade to the Knicks, however, never materialized. Instead, on November 23, he was shipped off to the hapless Buffalo Braves.

The surprising fact was that, in late 1977, there were still a few teams, Buffalo being one of them, that didn't have at least an educated guess that Bad News was an inveterate drug abuser masquerading as a professional athlete. In order to acquire him, along with a second- and a fourth-round draft pick, the Braves agreed to send their starting power forward, 6-foot-9 John Shumate, who was shooting 50 percent and averaging more than 15 points, former Spirit Gus Gerard, and a 1979 first-round draft choice to Detroit. Feldman, prodded by Barnes's highly publicized trade demand, had been able to pull off a swindle.

Fifteen

"LOSING HIS MIND" ON THE CELTICS BENCH

Following his trade to the Braves, Barnes was in no rush to report to his new club. Upset that he wouldn't be wearing a Knicks uniform and performing for the rabid fans inside Madison Square Garden, "The World's Most Famous Arena," he pouted for three days before arriving in Western New York.

In fact, thirty-six hours after he had been informed of the deal, Barnes was still in Detroit, attending a 76ers–Pistons game. Attired in all-black—including his trademark satin cape—he saluted his fans by taking a farewell lap around Cobo Arena, waving to the crowd, signing autographs, and high-fiving his gangster buddies in the stands. "Everyone on my team was wondering what the heck was going on," said then-Philadelphia guard Doug Collins. "We all knew Marvin was supposed to be on his way to Buffalo, but there he was at our game, putting on quite the show."

When Barnes finally made his way to the ice-crusted eastern shores of Lake Erie, more than 15,000 spectators packed Memorial Auditorium for his much-awaited debut as a Brave. As the crowd filed in, ushers handed out posters of him, with a banner headline above his picture that proclaimed, "Buffalo is Marvin's

Gardens." His talent and fascinating personality had, for that one game, provided him with superstar status.

During the 1976–77 season, new Braves owner John Y. Brown had sold off the contracts of his two top big men, Moses Malone and McAdoo, in order to raise enough capital to complete his purchase of the team. In the process, he had turned a very promising club into a laughingstock. Now, a year later, he was banking on the hope that Barnes could become Buffalo's primary inside scoring threat. That expectation proved to be a pipedream as the Braves' new starting power forward could do no better than average 11.8 points on 42 percent shooting.

Still, management had relatively few blowups with the flighty veteran, who seemed to have decent working relationships with everyone, from the owner to the coach, Lowell "Cotton" Fitzsimmons, to his teammates. "I kept the rule bending to a minimum," Barnes said. "I might have called in sick for two or three practices and showed up late for a few others, but nothing major."

Fitzsimmons, who would go on to be named NBA Coach of the Year in 1979 and '89, had a laidback style and communicated with his new starter through humor. On the road, the Hannibal, Missouri, native, who spoke with a twang, sometimes personally delivered Barnes's wake-up calls. "Time to rise and shine," he would shout into the phone. "Get excited, son. I want to see you go out and kick some butt today." He once even pretended to allow Bad News to call his own shots as far as playing time was concerned. "How many minutes you want tonight?" Fitzsimmons asked just before tipoff of a game against the Cleveland Cavs. "Do you want 20, 30, or 40, or should I just give you 10 because you were out partying last night? I'll just follow your orders."

"OK," Barnes replied, "I'll take all 48 'cause I'm going to score 60 and make you look like a genius."

The coach's upbeat approach made basketball enjoyable again for Bad News, whose off-court activities still very much revolved around dope and the nightclub scene.

One night at a local dive, the basketball star was introduced to a twenty-eight-year-old recording artist named Rick James, who had been raised in Buffalo and was seeking his big break in the music industry. At closing time, the entertainer invited Barnes to his grandmother's house, where the two shared some cocaine. As James talked about his goal to make a name for himself, he pulled out a cassette tape of one of his songs. "Want to hear it?" he asked. "It's called 'You and I.'"

As soon as the tape ended, Barnes said "Man, you're going to have a huge hit on your hands, guaranteed." Nine months later, "You and I" was released by Gordy Records, a Motown sub-label, and zoomed to number one on the *Billboard* rhythm and blues charts. The song made James a star and earned him the nickname "The Funk Punk."

It was the only time Barnes would see James, who, like himself, had been an addict his entire adult life. When the musician, who followed his first hit with the gold single "Super Freak," died of lung failure in 2004 at the age of fifty-six, nine different drugs—including Xanax, Valium, cocaine, heroin, marijuana, and ecstasy—were detected in his system. "All I could think about when I read about the autopsy results," Barnes said later in life, "was that God or luck must have been on my side because during any one of my binges, I could have gone out the exact same way Rick did."

After one of the Braves' many losses, John Y. Brown, who had made his fortune by building Kentucky Fried Chicken into a fast-food empire, confided to Barnes that he was working on a deal that would make NBA history. "All I can tell you right now," said the team owner, who would become the governor of Kentucky in 1979, "is that if it happens, you'll be a big part of it."

The secret details of the blockbuster transaction weren't unveiled until two months after Buffalo's 27–52 season had come to a merciful end. That's when the league announced that Brown had completed a franchise swap in which he traded the Braves, who would become the San Diego Clippers, for ownership of the Boston Celtics. As part of the complicated agreement, three of his Buffalo players—guards Nate "Tiny" Archibald and Billy Knight, along with Barnes—were sent to Boston for forwards Kermit Washington and Sidney Wicks, center Kevin Kunnert, and the rights to backcourt gunner Freeman Williams, who had been selected as the eighth overall pick of the 1978 draft by the Celtics.

After the unprecedented exchange of teams had been approved by the league, Brown summoned Barnes, who would be accompanied by Debbe, to Las Vegas for a private meeting.

"Got a proposition for you," the proud new owner of pro sports' most successful franchise told Barnes as soon as they sat down for dinner at the Sands Hotel. "It's something that's never been done. First of all, I'm prepared to pay you 70 percent of your deferred payments from the Braves and Celtics right now. It's money that I don't have to start giving you for six more years. That alone should show I have faith in you.

"Here's the second part of my offer: I want to remove all the guarantees, except the injury clause, from your contract. That means if you start screwing up, I can cut you. I have to know you're going to give me your all. I'm asking you to take a risk and prove to me you're still a great player. If you accept my terms, I'll add an incentive clause to the contract. Get me 10 rebounds a night, and you'll make an extra $40,000. Get me 12, and I'll throw in another $60,000."

Bad News wasn't quite sold on the proposal, so Brown sweetened the pot.

"Tell you what, I'll give you a $100,000 signing bonus if you agree to random drug testing," said John Y. "There've been rumors floating around about you using cocaine. I want to make sure you're not involved with that stuff. If you refuse to be tested, then the bonus gets cut in half."

Looking Brown in the eyes and without any indecision, Barnes replied, "Fifty grand sounds like a good number to me. You got yourself a deal." The contract provisions were hastily handwritten on a cocktail napkin and a casino promotional brochure, signed by both parties, witnessed by the hotel's general manager, Xeroxed, and faxed to the Celtics office, where team counsel Jan Volk struggled to decipher the scrawled agreement.

En route to the East Coast, Marvin and Debbe flew to Austin, Texas, for a visit with his "business associate," Hindelang, who was part-owner of the Tree House Grill, a trendy local restaurant. During their stay, the couple was married at a City Hall ceremony.

While the newlyweds honeymooned, John Y. arranged for them to rent a two-bedroom suite at Longfellow Place, overlooking the dirty water of the Charles River and just up the block from the historic rat's nest known as the Boston Garden. Living next to the Barnes family would be the Celtics owner and his wife, Phyllis George, who had been crowned Miss America in 1971.

Boston's coach for the 1978–79 season was Tom "Satch" Sanders, an even-tempered former Celtics forward who had been known for his defensive prowess. He had the reputation of treating players with respect, calling each one of them "Mister," and never resorting to screaming or cursing as motivational tools. Barnes, who began the season as the team's sixth man, initially got along well with his coach because he was putting up impressive numbers, having accumulated 25 points, 13 rebounds, five steals, and three blocks in the first two games of the season. Hometown fans were cheering so loudly for him that rookie forward Cedric Maxwell told the media, "If Marvin keeps playing like this, he'll own this city."

Feeling like a big shot, Bad News decided to bring along six of his old friends from ACI when the team flew down to New York for a Wednesday night game against the Knicks. He booked reservations for his "Dirty Half-Dozen" on the team's flights and gave all his guests enough money to buy ties and sports jackets so they would blend in with how the Celtics players were dressed. Years later, Boston teammate Don Chaney would jokingly state that Barnes, who recorded eight points, 10 rebounds, three steals, and three blocks in 26 minutes that night, deserved credit for being the first NBA player to have an entourage.

But the magnetism of drugs quickly sucked in the Celtics' newest folk hero. "I became so hooked that while I was sitting at the end of the bench during a game at the Garden, I put a towel over my head, reached into the pocket of my warm-ups, pulled out a vial filled with coke, and snorted up. A second later, I looked down and saw blood dripping out of my nose."

When Chaney, who was sitting next to the distracted forward, noticed what was happening, he scooted to an empty seat near the Boston coaching staff. "I looked over at Marvin and did a double-take," he remembers. "I thought he had lost his mind."

Still, the veteran guard didn't say a word to anyone about what he had witnessed. "Remember, I was a teammate of Marvin in St. Louis. He was a wild man back then, so nothing he ever did came as a complete shock to me."

Barnes's relationship with Sanders deteriorated during a four-game road trip in late October, after the reserve power forward had received a panic-stricken call from his mother, who complained that she was experiencing health problems. She also informed him that his sister had been arrested for robbery and was facing a possible ten-year sentence due to her extensive criminal history, which included felony convictions for drug conspiracy, receiving stolen goods, and cashing bad checks. When Marvin phoned Alfreda, who was free on bail, he could hear fear in her voice as she begged him to come to Providence. "You've got to help me find a good lawyer," she pleaded. "If I go back into the system, I won't be coming out alive. I've got too many enemies on the inside. I need you here, please."

When Marvin sought permission to go home, Sanders denied the request. "You're telling me your mother has a heart ailment," the coach said. "You're not a doctor, are you? And you're telling me your sister has major legal issues. You don't have a law degree, do you? There's nothing you can do for either of them by going to Providence. You can help them by making a few simple phone calls. You can get in touch with a good cardiologist and make an appointment for your mother. You can wire money to your sister for an attorney. I'm sure you must know a good one who will take her case. I'm telling you straight out, Mr. Barnes, if you go home, you're through as a Celtic." After much soul searching, Bad News reluctantly remained with the team.

Two weeks later, Sanders found himself in a no-win situation during a Celtics–Pistons contest at the Garden. He had just been ordered by John Y. Brown to play Barnes and teammate Billy Knight a minimum of 40 minutes a game.

"Marvin did some fabulous things on the court for the first five minutes that night. Then he became exhausted and began to jog instead of run," Sanders recalls. "After another two minutes, he started walking up and down the court, waving his arms back and forth as a signal for me to bring in a sub. I had no choice but to take him out. Knight was also gassed, so I gave him a rest, too.

"I looked across the court to where the owner was sitting and saw that his face had turned beet red. Then I watched him storm down an exit ramp. I told my assistant, KC Jones, that I thought we were in deep trouble. KC looked at me and, with a straight face, replied, 'What, um, you mean we, kimosabe?' I could tell from John Y.'s temper tantrum that I was about to become the 'ex-coach' of the Boston Celtics. Sure enough, the next day I got the proverbial axe."

Brown, who was so egotistical that he truly believed he knew more about running a team than legendary Celtics General Manager Red Auerbach, replaced Sanders, whose record for the season had been 2–12, with thirty-year-old All-Star center Dave Cowens, who became player-coach. The move received Barnes's unconditional support. "Both Dave and I were madmen when it came to competing." he later said. "We both hustled, we both liked to run the court, and we both played a physical game. I thought we'd click."

Despite all the good vibes Barnes felt about team chemistry, he continued to use drugs on a daily basis, purchasing cocaine from a dealer named Al, who worked out of a rundown saloon in a raunchy downtown area of the city known as "the Combat Zone."

"I was hanging around him so much, Marvin said, "that my wife started accusing me of turning homosexual."

Troubled by Barnes's increasingly odd behavior, John Y. decided to confront him. In a face-off straight out of *The Godfather*, the two met in a darkened booth in the back of Polcari's, a fashionable Italian restaurant in Boston's North End. The team owner began the conversation by assuring the headstrong power forward that he was still a believer. "But don't screw with me," Brown said. "If you're using cocaine, I'm telling you to flush it all down the toilet. We talked about this before. I never should have offered you a bonus unless you were willing to be drug tested. That was a big mistake on my part, but keep in mind that I can cut you today if I want because you gave up all your [contractual] guarantees."

The explicit threat had no effect on Barnes, who continued to lead the life of a conniving dope fiend no matter the risks or consequences. In fact, he was in such a dazed state that even Al the coke dealer took it upon himself to offer some unsolicited advice. "You've got to cut way back on the blow. You look like garbage, and you're playing like garbage," he told his best customer, who was half-listening while snorting a line of cocaine that had been provided free of charge. "If you don't get your act together, that Brown character is going to dump your ass. You can bank on it."

A few days later, Debbe gave her husband an ultimatum. "It's either me or the damn drugs," she said. "Make up your mind."

With no hesitation, Marvin callously replied, "OK, it's the drugs."

An hour later, Debbe and three-year-old Tiffani were packed and on their way back to Providence.

Having spent more than $600 a week for his drug buys, Barnes was down to his last $50. "I was so short on cash that I signed a $5,000 endorsement deal to wear Pony basketball shoes even though I didn't like how they fit me. But for that much money, I would have worn flip-flops on the court."

Throughout December, Barnes produced surprisingly exceptional stats, scoring in double-digits nine times, including 20 points in a home victory versus the Clippers on December 6, 22 points (along with 10 rebounds and three steals) in a 121–105 win against the Pacers at Boston Garden two weeks later, and a season-high 29 points (plus eight rebounds and two steals) on December 27, in a 112–103 triumph over the Kansas City Kings at the Checkerdome in St. Louis before a crowd of 14,442. "That game was my homecoming," Barnes said years later.

"When I stepped onto the court, my old Spirits fans gave me a two minute-long ovation, and then I put on an exhibition that amazed even me."

Despite having demonstrated his prodigious talent, Barnes once again sabotaged himself. A week after the Celtics had returned from St. Louis, he failed to show up for two practices, which resulted in a one-game suspension.

With Boston's chances of making the playoffs diminishing rapidly, it became clear that the team was going to release either the irrepressible Barnes or 6-foot-6½ Earl Williams—who had been on injured reserve for a month after complaining of excruciating lower back pain—in order to reduce payroll costs. Two days before Cowens planned to make his decision on which player to cut, he held a morning shootaround at the Boston Garden.

"As I got out of my car, I spotted Williams walking ahead of me in the parking lot. Earl was walking perfectly normal—until he entered the building," Cowens said. "Then he started limping badly and taking baby steps. After practice, I met with Auerbach and told him what I had witnessed. Red gave me the go-ahead to cut the guy. Before our game that night, I confronted Williams in front of most of the players and told him he was released.

"I think what happened," says Volk, the Celtics team counsel, "is that someone must have told Earl that the team could not cut an injured player. He mistakenly thought a back problem would force us to keep him. What he failed to understand was that an injury didn't mean we couldn't cut him because of what is referred to in the collective bargaining agreement as a 'lack of skills.'"

Thanks to Williams's pathetic attempt to deceive his coach and teammates, Barnes remained a Celtic. Still experiencing cash flow problems, he asked Cowens if he could be excused from practice the following day in order to resolve a major financial issue.

"Don't even think about it," the fuming coach said. "Don't you realize how lucky you are to still be on this team?"

The willful backup forward skipped the workout anyway and caught a flight to St. Louis for an emergency meeting with Becton. "I needed to get my hands on $5,000," Barnes said. "That's what I thought I'd need to buy enough coke to last me for the rest of the season. As usual, Patch came through for me."

Instead of being released upon his return to Boston, Barnes was slapped with another suspension, this time for two games. "I didn't care. I had my money and I had my drugs. Nothing else mattered to me."

Though Bad News had ducked a pair of bullets, he would not be able to dodge a third.

During the final week of January 1979, Barnes, claiming he was suffering from a debilitating mystery illness whose on-again, off-again symptoms included fevers, headaches, dizziness, and nausea, missed three consecutive games and two more practices. Thomas Silva, the team physician, strongly urged him to get a complete checkup at Massachusetts General Hospital. The "bedridden" forward, however, claimed he was "feeling too weak" to undergo testing.

An indignant Cowens met with John Y. Brown and told him, "There's nothing wrong with poor Marvin. What he's doing is quitting on his teammates. You can force me keep him on the roster, but he'll never play another minute for me."

On February 7, 1979, Barnes was ordered to clean out his locker. "You're through here," Cowens said. "I'm done with you."

The farewell speech produced no reaction whatsoever.

"I'd been dope sick for two weeks straight," Barnes said years later. "There was no way I could play or practice, so I kept dreaming up phony illnesses. I never blamed the Celtics for getting rid of me. If I had been the coach, I'd have gotten rid of me, too."

Thanks to Becton's generosity, the out-of-work athlete had a sufficient bankroll to last him a minimum of five weeks. At least that's how Bad News calculated his budget for the necessities of life—cocaine, heroin, weed, and whatever other drug he might be able to acquire.

Cowens had no misgivings about his decision. "After I cut Marvin, he didn't say a word because he knew how badly he had screwed up. Deep down, he was really a good guy. He just wasn't dependable. I couldn't prove that he was using drugs, but I had a real strong hunch because he was always acting so nutty—like the time he was sitting in the stands for the entire pregame warm-ups, holding a baby, posing for pictures, and signing autographs. It was as if he was totally oblivious we were about to play an NBA game. I had to personally go up to him and remind him that he had a job to do.

"The sad thing is that the guy had a boatload of talent. He was both powerful and smooth, half Connie Hawkins and half Alex English. When he got himself geared up to play, he could do it all and make it look easy. But you never knew what you were going to get from him. He could give you a double-double, or he could stink up the place. As a first-year coach, I needed players I could at least count on to give me a full effort every single game."

Barnes's time with the Celtics totaled only 38 games. His averages: 8.1 points and 4.7 rebounds.

Once his hopped-up brain began to unscramble, Bad News was able to comprehend the negative consequences of being released by Boston. It suddenly dawned on him that the remaining two-plus years of his long-term contract were now null and void due to the terms of the "napkin contract" he had signed with Brown in Vegas the previous summer. "When I got cut, I was flat out loopy. For the sake of getting high whenever I felt like it, I threw away somewhere around four hundred grand."

Besides being unemployed, Barnes faced another major problem, one unrelated to basketball. A day after the Celtics had officially released him, agents from the DEA and the FBI knocked on his apartment door, seeking to question him about his knowledge of a drug trafficking ring that ran its business out of Florida and Missouri. Grudgingly consenting to be interviewed, the squirming athlete was grilled for more than two hours concerning his relationship with Becton and Hindelang.

"I played dumb. I told them I knew nothing about no drug operation. That's when this one guy who looked like Clark Kent, with the horned-rimmed glasses, the bulging chest and the buttoned-up sports coat, opened a two-foot-high cardboard box and dumped everything in it onto my dining room table."

"Take a good look at all this evidence. You're waist deep in shit," the FBI agent said while shoving documents, audio tapes, and photographs in front of Barnes. "The worst thing you could do is try to jerk us around."

Then the DEA investigator chimed in. "We know you're lying because we've got statements from eyewitnesses that put you in a St. Louis restaurant discussing business with Becton and Hindelang. We also have film of you with a half-dozen other known drug traffickers. And we can prove you're full of it because we wiretapped phone conversations between you and your man, Patch. The next time we come after you, it will be in a court of law. If you get on the witness stand and swear you don't have any knowledge about Becton's operation, you'll do five years, minimum, in a federal penitentiary. That's our guarantee to you."

Barnes, however, was offered a way out. "We believe you have information which could be useful to our investigation," he was told. "You come clean, work with us, and you can walk away scot free, without anyone ever knowing you talked to us."

There was, however, no way Barnes was about to become a stoolie by ratting out his friends. Moments after the G-men had left, he walked to a pay phone two blocks away on Causeway Street and called Becton to inform him of the agents' visit. The next day Becton flew to Boston and met with Barnes at a tavern on Friend Street. "The feds are bluffing. Don't worry about them," the mob boss said. "They just wanted to see how much you knew about my organization. If they come after you again, stick with what you've told them: You don't know me well, and you don't know a thing about my business. Understand?"

About the only thing Barnes understood was that he was being squeezed. "Those guys, they've got all kinds of proof that I'm real tight with you and Hindelang. Tell me why I should keep on lying and end up in prison."

"Because you owe me, that's why," Becton replied. "How many times have I bailed you out of jams you got into all by yourself? Just play things smart, for Christ's sake, and stop panicking. If you ever do get charged with anything, which I swear won't happen, you're going to keep your mouth shut and do your fucking time."

Sixteen

"STUCK ON STUPID" FOR ALMOST A YEAR

Unhinged by the pointed threats made to him by both Becton and the federal agents, Barnes retreated to his mother's house in March of 1979 and went on a hunt for drugs, quickly hooking up with local pushers from his past.

During his first month back in Providence, he was snorting cocaine two or three times a day, either at nightclubs or alone in cheap, dingy hotel rooms. As his tolerance level for the drug increased, the euphoria he experienced from getting high diminished. "I went from using two or three grams a day to five or six. After a while, coke just wasn't getting the job done no matter how much I did. I needed a more intense rush, so I started snorting heroin. Using that crap got me stuck on stupid for almost a year.

"Once you get all messed up on smack the way I did, the only way to kick the habit is to go cold turkey. With heroin, there's no such thing as easing yourself off it. You either suffer through withdrawal or you keep on using. Every time I tried to quit, I'd puke my guts out and get muscle pains that were so bad that I'd be all curled up in a ball, screaming like a banshee. I was too damn weak-willed to live through a week of hell, so I always ended up going straight back to using the stuff."

Fearful that the feds were going to show up at his mother's door at any moment and place him in handcuffs, Barnes soon moved on to Detroit, where he planned to hide out so deep in the ghetto that an entire government task force wouldn't be able to locate him. On his first day in town, he managed to find a safe haven on the East Side of the city, moving in with Inez "Mama" Baxter and her family. He had first met the middle-aged housewife while playing with the Pistons. She was a self-sacrificing, God-fearing woman whom many teammates had hired to babysit their children. While Marvin was staying with her, Mama cooked his meals, washed his clothes, and took him along with her family to Sunday church services.

And for a few fleeting weeks, life was uncomplicated.

But a loud knock at the Baxters' door one Saturday morning changed all that. Standing on the front stoop were Johnny "Little Man" Curry and Leo "Big Man" Curry, twins whom Barnes knew from his playing days in Detroit. "The Curry Boys," as they were known by every veteran Detroit beat cop, asked if he would be interested in hanging out with them and their crew. Marvin knew better than to decline the invitation. The two violent drug honchos were branded as being vengeful assassins and, according to retired FBI agent Gregg Schwarz, that reputation was not undeserved.

The brothers were the leaders of a highly structured organization that sold all the cocaine on the city's East Side. Although their enterprise, unlike Becton's, was not nationwide in scope, the Curry Boys were by far the most powerful and vindictive gangsters in the metropolitan area. "Give them a reason to suspect that one of their rivals was attempting to muscle in on their turf, and they'd make sure the competition was eliminated permanently,"

Schwarz says. "And they'd make sure everyone knew exactly who had given the orders."

Because Becton and his top associates were under investigation, Barnes's money supply had dried up. No longer was he receiving monthly "royalties" from his boss. The beleaguered St. Louis drug trafficker, in fact, had shut down his once-untouchable operation until he could be satisfied the feds were not going to file charges against him. The only way Bad News could obtain ready access to drugs was to become the Curry Boys' sidekick. Each day he rode shotgun in Little Man's metallic red Excalibur as the drug distributor supervised his crew of eager-to-please "nose candy" salesmen. As the pair drove from one location to the next, they were followed by two, sometimes three carloads of armed bodyguards and barrel-chested debt collectors. The Currys were cautious and intelligent. Not once did Barnes witness them handle cash or "merchandise" as they talked in whispers with their minions.

Little Man, who bore a striking resemblance to the rock star Prince, provided Barnes with a place to stay at his home, where the former Piston was given permission to help himself to a stash of cocaine that was kept in a compartment underneath the bottom shelf of a tool cabinet.

After two months, though, the convenient living arrangement came to an end. Tipped off by a high-ranking Detroit police officer who was on the Curry Boys' payroll that the gang was about to be taken down by the FBI and DEA, Little Man handed his houseguest $500 and told him it would be a smart move to skip town.

Although Barnes was never a person of interest in the FBI investigation, an ironclad case had been built against the Curry twins, two of their brothers, and sixteen other members of their organization. Even Little Man's wife, Cathy, the niece of then–Detroit Mayor Coleman Young, was suspected of having a role in the operation.

From the time the FBI began its probe in 1979, it took four years to wrap up the case. When a grand jury was impaneled, the US Attorney's office introduced evidence of thirty witness statements, surveillance films, and secretly recorded conversations among members of the gang. On one of the tapes, the Curry Boys were heard arguing about which one of them was the "most treacherous mother fucker in all of Detroit."

FBI agent Schwarz testified at a bail hearing that the twins were aware their every move was being scrutinized by federal agents because they had been given inside information by a "friend of the family," who worked as a supervisor at the Detroit police command center. The FBI investigator said Little Man, knowing that evidence was being gathered to bring down the organization, was caught on tape telling his sister to "continue to do business, but be discreet."

On the day the most publicized drug trial in Detroit history was scheduled to begin, Little Man asked Schwarz if a last-minute plea deal might be arranged. "The best I can do for you is to recommend twenty-year sentences and $250,000 fines for you and Leo," the dogged lawman said. "Of course, you can take your chances at trial, but we've got you cold. Trust me, you could end up doing forty years because we have all the proof needed to convict you, your twin, and everyone on your payroll."

On the spot, the Curry twins accepted the offer. They ended up serving thirteen years and three months of their twenty-year sentences for tax evasion and operating a continuing criminal enterprise. As the pair was being led out of court, Schwarz and his partner, Herman Groman, who had been sitting directly behind the prosecutor, mockingly waved goodbye to them. Little Man smiled, raised his handcuffed hands, and wiggled his fingers at the two FBI agents.

There were eighteen other members of the Curry Boys' drug ring who were co-defendants that day, all of whom were paraded before the judge. Each one accepted plea deals that resulted in substantial prison time.

After fleeing Detroit in July of 1979, Barnes drove to St. Louis to reunite with Becton. It was the first time he had seen the drug kingpin in more than a year, and he wasn't confident he still had his mentor's trust after having become rattled by the feds when they had confronted him in Boston. With a smile and a hug, Patch assured his one-time apprentice that he was still in his good graces.

"You'll always be my compadre," he said. "Besides, I think I'm in the clear. If the FBI thought they had a case against me, something would have gone down by now. I know you're here for a reason, Marvin. How much you looking for? All I can spare right now is a couple grand. I'll send you more when I can. Until then, lay low."

On the trip home to Providence, Barnes attempted to estimate how much cash Becton had given him through the years, not including the $1.5 million he had earned as a minor partner in the drug trafficking ring. By his calculations, the St. Louis gangster had forked over more than $400,000 to bail him out of his never-ending series of personal crises.

"I've got to set the record straight," Barnes said. "Patch never encouraged me to use cocaine, heroin, or even weed. Because of my connections, I had easy access to every drug known to man. Getting hooked and staying hooked was all on me. I convinced myself that I could stop at any time, but I just kept telling myself there was no pressing reason to quit. That's how addicts justify their habits. We're all weak-minded."

It was mid-September of 1979, and Barnes was certain he would never get another opportunity to play in the NBA.

He was mistaken.

Unexpectedly, Gene Shue, who had become head coach of the San Diego Clippers, phoned to offer the now sickly-looking 175-pound power forward a tryout. Broke and fantasizing that through an act of God he could instantaneously shed his addictions, Barnes accepted the invitation. But after only four days of mini-camp, Shue had seen enough, cutting the broken down free agent, who had been thoroughly outplayed and out-hustled by a bunch of raw, undrafted rookies.

Six hours after arriving back in Providence, the castoff started binging on heroin with an old friend from his ACI days, a junkie named Sam, who had injected so much black tar heroin into his veins that his arms looked as if they had been attacked by a swarm of wasps. "Just looking at him gave me the heebie-jeebies. Real nasty-looking sight," Bad News said. "He had thousands of scabby red puncture marks, from his arm pits right down to his fingertips. His mind was shot. I'd be talking to him and he'd wander off to the bathroom to get high. He'd come back bleeding from his arms, hands shaking, eyes as big as saucers. I thought for sure I was looking at a dead man walking."

Not that Barnes was much better off. Searching for that "next score" was his constant and lone objective, even though he knew his addiction was getting ready to swallow him whole. "My brain was turning to mush. I couldn't live with heroin, and I damn sure couldn't live without it."

Trapped in what he perceived to be a no-win situation, Barnes concluded that his very existence had become worthless.

On a November night in 1979, he checked into a fleabag motel off Interstate 95 in North Providence, plopped onto a bed, pulled out two packets of heroin from his jacket pocket, and began to snort up. At his side was a silver-plated pistol that he stared at for an hour straight, trying to muster the guts to end the madness. Sometime around midnight, he phoned his ex-wife Debbe and confessed to her that he was a trigger squeeze away from killing himself. After hearing his chilling words, she pleaded with him to get help and, after much convincing, persuaded him to drive to her house.

For the next week, she and her siblings, as well as their parents, took turns providing round-the-clock care and encouragement as Barnes struggled to break loose from heroin's stranglehold. The first thirty-six hours were relatively manageable as he still had a substantial amount of the drug in his system. By day three, however, his entire body had shut down. He shivered, broke out into cold sweats, drooled uncontrollably, and frequently retched as a reflex action to the burning stomach cramps that literally took his breath away. All the while, depression and anxiety were playing cruel tricks on his psyche.

"It was supreme payback for all the times I'd snorted up. What I went through was worse than Chinese water torture. I was positive that I was going insane."

The agonizing ordeal jolted Barnes back into sobriety—for the time being.

Shortly after New Year's, Shue, desperate for frontcourt help, called again, offering a 10-day contract to the same underachiever he had cut four months earlier. "Don't ask me why I wanted Marvin so badly. I always liked him as a person, and I kept remembering what an awesome talent he had once been," said the two-time NBA Coach of the Year. "I thought if I could motivate him to be just a third of the player he was during his first two years as a pro, he might help us win some games—perhaps enough to get us into the playoffs."

Devoid of confidence, Barnes received permission to mull over the offer for a day and immediately flew St. Louis to consult with Becton. They met in an out-of-business furniture store where the drug wholesaler was negotiating a dope deal with an out-of-town customer. The three men then walked to the basement, which was filled with 5,000 pounds of marijuana. While the prospective buyer sampled the goods, the two old friends discussed the job opportunity with the Clippers.

"I haven't touched a basketball in four months. If I go to San Diego now, I'll just end up being cut in a few days. No sense looking bad," said Barnes. "My best move would be to ask for a fresh start in training camp next season."

The spineless excuse-making enraged Becton. "You're talking ragtime. Listen, you ain't no big star no more. This is your last chance. Personally, I think the coach is doing you a huge favor. He knows you're a total fuck-up, but he's still willing to give you a shot. It's not as if you're an old man. You're only twenty-seven. Call him up and tell him you'll be there tomorrow, ready to practice. Grow some balls, for Christ's sake."

When Barnes arrived in San Diego, he phoned Shue and asked if he could wait a week before signing. "Gene, I'm not in game shape," he said. "Give me a little time to get my wind back." Before hanging up, the NBA retread mentioned he was facing a slight cash flow problem. "Coach, I'm tapped out. Can you help me out a little?" he pleaded.

Shue assigned one of his assistants, Don Moran, to be the "rusty" forward's personal trainer on a full-time basis for two weeks. He also dispatched a front office intern to drop off a $1,000 salary advance to ease the player's financial bind. Although Barnes had been clean for almost a month and a half, he could barely keep up with his forty-six-year-old workout taskmaster as they went through their daily routine of calisthenics, shooting drills, wind sprints, and a three-mile run. But Moran was a combination master motivator and drill sergeant. By the time the intensive conditioning sessions had ended, the twenty-seven-year-old reclamation project at least looked like a basketball warrior, lean and strong, with a bounce in his step. The issue was: Could he still play the game with any degree of effectiveness?

Because the deadline for teams to offer 10-day contracts had passed, Barnes was signed for the remainder of the season, with his minimum-salaried contract automatically being fully guaranteed.

During his first week with the team, he struck up a friendship with his former college rival and now San Diego teammate Bill Walton, who had led the Portland Trail Blazers to a NBA championship in 1977. Before long, the former number-one draft pick was inviting Barnes to his and his wife Susie's house almost every night for dinner. On the road, the two players spent hours swapping stories about their rather extreme off-the-court experiences.

The Clippers had a number of other quirky characters on their 1979–80 roster, including Joe "Jellybean" Bryant, Kobe's father, and guard Lloyd B. Free, the team's leading scorer.

Bryant was a 6-foot-9 forward who possessed the ballhandling abilities of a point guard. Prior to being traded to San Diego in '79, he had spent four seasons with the 76ers, having averaged 6.4 points a game as a bench fill-in for All-Stars Julius Erving and George McGinnis. Now, as member of the Clippers, he was determined to prove that his shake-and-bake moves had been underutilized in Philly. "Good guy but goofy, just like his nickname," Barnes said later. "Loved to show off for the fans. He'd get the ball and go into his one-on-one thing, dribbling between his legs and behind his back. As he was doing all of this, he'd be smiling at the crowd and talking trash to the guy who was guarding him."

"Joe could be a handful at times," said Bryant's 76ers teammate Steve Mix. "He was a magician with the ball, but what held him back was that he didn't have a reliable outside jumper. But that never stopped him from bombing away whenever he got the chance."

Free was a fearless and clutch long-distance gunner whose game day routine included downing three or four Budweiser Kings a couple hours before tipoff. "Swear to God, the man played half smashed, sweating like a bull as he ran up and down the court. Didn't hurt his game none," Barnes said. "He'd score 25, 30 every game, chucking from out deep. And the guy had the funkiest shooting motion I've ever seen. To begin with, he'd release the ball way up by his right ear. Then he'd put a ridiculously high arc on every one of his shots. They just sort of floated through the air for a couple of seconds and dropped straight through the net."

Unlike Free, Barnes was feeling the pressure to produce. "Deep down, I knew I had been given a gift. I didn't deserve to be on that team. My reflexes were shot and I had no spring in my legs. Hate to admit it, but there were times when I was praying I wouldn't have to take off my warm-ups and go in. If I shot 50 percent in a game and got three or four rebounds, it was a good night."

Going into the final three games of the season, the Clippers had a slim chance of gaining a playoff berth if they could beat the Trail Blazers at home and then upset both the Lakers and Suns on the road. In the matchup against Portland, Barnes was on the court for the final 28 seconds, with his team trailing by a point. On an inbounds play, the ball came into Free on the left wing. Everyone on the court anticipated that the guard with no conscience would go one-on-one and launch the deciding shot. Instead, he passed the ball inside to Barnes, who was wide open in the lane, with plenty of time to square up, aim, and fire. His shot, however, never reached the rim. "I completely choked," he said afterwards. "Five feet from the basket and I put up a three-foot jumper." The air ball cost the Clippers the game and eliminated them from playoff contention.

The embarrassing flub would be Barnes's final play in the NBA.

The following evening, as the Clippers were warming up to face the Lakers, Shue asked the humbled forward if he wanted to start. "This is a chance to show people you deserve to be in this league," the coach said. The offer, however, was politely declined. "I appreciate what you're trying to do," Barnes said, "but I'm not the player I used to be. I don't want to go out there and hurt the team again. Do me a favor, Gene, keep me on the bench from here on out."

"For the first time in my career," said Barnes, who shot a career-low 40 percent from the field and averaged only 3.2 points and 3.6 rebounds during his 20-game stint with San Diego, "I felt I had no right to be on the court."

Seventeen

ON THE ROAD TO NOWHERE

Bad News Barnes's NBA career stats weren't exactly Springfield, Massachusetts, material. In his four seasons (171 games), he had averaged 9.2 points on 44-percent shooting. His rebounding had been equally as unimpressive at 5.5 a game.[1]

Despite his four-year "slump," the twenty-eight-year-old forward found employment for the 1980–81 season when he was pursued by a team from the seaport city of Trieste, Italy, located four and a half miles from the Yugoslavian border. The club's owners, who had deep pockets, were looking to add a big-name American center or power forward, someone with substantial pro experience. Barnes, despite his checkered past and atrocious recent play, evidently fit the team's needs because the management of Hurlingham Trieste, which normally played one game per week during the regular season, signed him to a contract that provided an exceedingly generous salary of $15,000 a month tax-free, plus use of a new car and a modern two-bedroom apartment.

Having a month to wait until his departure date, Barnes flew to New York, where he stayed with one of his former drug

---

1   In his two ABA seasons, Barnes shot 50 percent from the floor and averaged 24 points with 13.4 rebounds and 1.9 blocks.

suppliers, an addict named Claude, who had recently purchased a large jar of potent heroin.

Overcome by an acute case of brainlock, Bad News figured there could be no possible harm in sampling the drug for a few weeks. Eager to make a small buy but, as usual, lacking funds, he devised a plan that might provide him with as much as $70,000.

Beginning in 1982, the Spirits ownership group would be obligated to start paying deferred compensation to Barnes that totaled $156,000. Disinclined to wait that long, he phoned Schupak and inquired whether a settlement might be arranged. The attorney for the Silna brothers told Marvin to stop by his office in Manhattan to discuss the matter. When Barnes, accompanied by Claude, arrived for the meeting, Schupak sensed Barnes's anxiety and opted to play hardball, offering a meager $25,000 in severance.

With an eye on the prize (the jar of high-grade heroin), Barnes didn't even attempt to negotiate a more equitable resolution. "I'll take it, but I'll need it all in cash money by tomorrow morning." In effect, he had signed off on a deal that paid him only 16 cents on the dollar of what he would have received in deferred payments.

By the time basketball's master of mayhem arrived in Italy, drug purchases had trimmed his $25,000 bankroll in half. Moving into a comfortable hillside apartment that offered a panoramic view of two majestic cathedrals and a nineteenth-century fortress, Barnes was able to find a reliable source for drugs during his first night on foreign soil. Another player from the US, 6-foot-5 Rich Laurel, a 1977 fifth-round draft pick of the San Antonio Spurs whose NBA career lasted only 12 games before he was waived, introduced his new teammate to three acquaintances, all male models whose sideline work was peddling cocaine and heroin.

The CEO of the flourishing local operation was twenty-six-year-old playboy Ricardo Dainese, who went by the nickname "Ricky the Pirate." Naturally, it didn't take long for Trieste's newest sports icon to cultivate a close and rewarding friendship with the debonair drug distributor.

The relationship, however, was short-lived. A month and a half into the Italian League's schedule, Barnes's paid vacation came to an inglorious end when he was released after missing three practices in one week.

Two days after his contract had been terminated, Barnes stopped by Dainese's cottage to refill his coke supply. As soon as he knocked on the front door, three men, all carrying Uzi machine guns, came charging out of the bushes that lined the perimeter of the property. It appeared as if they were there to ambush Ricky and steal his money and drugs. Instead, they began shouting, "Policia, Policia."

Because he wasn't high or in possession of any dope, Barnes was relieved to know they were cops, not thieves or mobsters. Taken into custody and whisked away to the city jail, he was interrogated by Trieste's police chief, who asked him whether he had ever witnessed Dainese selling drugs. "Nope," he replied. "Just got here eight weeks ago. I've only met the man a couple times."

Refusing to believe the denial, the city's top cop stuck his nose to within three inches of his captive's face and loudly repeated his question. "Look," Barnes shouted, "I don't know what the hell you're talking about, so stop all the hollering. You ain't dealing with no punk-ass kid."

Annoyed that the American wouldn't implicate Dainese in a drug dealing scheme, the chief summoned a deputy to escort the uncooperative detainee down a set of cobblestone steps that led to a primitive damp dungeon. While being forcibly shoved along, Bad News stopped dead in his tracks when he came face to face with five convicts, all Charles Manson look-alikes, staring blankly at him from behind bars. "You might as well shoot me right here and now," he told the officer, "'cause I ain't going nowhere near those freaks."

After a brief standoff, the guard ushered Barnes to a different cell, where Ricky the Pirate, two other Italians, and three Africans were being held.

Meals in the dark cave-like jail were barely digestible: over-salted scrambled eggs and fatty half-cooked sausage for breakfast; cold pasta for lunch; and some type of watery goulash, which smelled like rotten hamburger, at dinner time. "We got the same lousy food every day I was there. It looked like the slop that's fed to pigs."

While the guards were upstairs taking a break, one of the inmates opened a small cardboard box and tipped it over onto the bare floor. Out tumbled a dozen different kinds of prescription medicines, perhaps 500 tablets in all. The assortment included Percodan, codeine, tranquilizers, and Vicodin.

No one explained how the narcotics had been smuggled in. Barnes simply presumed a fellow prisoner had bribed a jailer. For four days, he ate only rock-hard bread, surviving the ordeal by drinking water and gulping down a wide variety of pills.

Tipped off by a guard that he was about to be charged with making false statements to a law enforcement official, an offense that carried a possible 10-year sentence in Italy, Barnes requested and received permission to phone an attorney in Rhode Island. After making contact, he appealed for help. "Talk to the US embassy here," he said. "Tell them I need to see somebody right now. Let them know I'm being railroaded, that the cops here have me locked away in some stinking dungeon."

A State Department envoy arrived at the jail the following afternoon and demanded that the American basketball player be released until a formal complaint was brought against him. As soon as Barnes was temporarily set free, the diplomat offered some advice. "US citizens don't normally get a fair shake in the courts here. This is off the record, but if I were you, I'd sneak out of the country right away, today if possible. They won't come after you for such a questionable charge."

And with that, Barnes rushed to his apartment, packed his suitcases, and phoned for a cab. He was driven to the tiny village of Monrupino, a quarter of a mile from the Yugoslavian border. From there, he fled on foot, trudging through a dense forest until he reached the town of Sezana in the state of Slovenia. After taking a one-hour bus ride to a two-runway airport, the fugitive from Italian justice boarded a prop plane to Frankfurt, Germany, where he caught a connecting flight to New York.

Once back in the States, Barnes, now a wanted man in Trieste, phoned Laurel to recount his experiences while on the lam. His former teammate explained that, in actuality, the case against Ricky the Pirate involved much more than a drug charge. It seemed Dainese was also being investigated for extortion. It was alleged that during the wild parties at his home, he had taken nude photographs and X-rated films of nearly fifty doped-up females, some as young as fifteen. They were the daughters of politicians, entertainers, and corporate CEOs. According to police, their suspect was planning on using his private porn collection to blackmail the young women's wealthy parents, which he had estimated would net him a fortune. As soon as the media learned details of the supposed bribery plot, it became a major scandal throughout Italy.

As the summer of 1981 approached, Barnes, who had been in and out of rehab four times since his return from Italy, had no plans for another long shot bid to win a spot on an NBA roster. But as had been the case so many times on his road to nowhere, along came another true believer to offer a lift. Larry Brown, who was now coaching the New Jersey Nets, invited him to play for his team in the Los Angeles Summer League. At the time, the LA Pro-Am was so highly regarded that almost every NBA club sent a squad of veterans, draft picks, and free agents to participate in the two-week showcase. The basketball drifter was promised that if he performed well, a one-year $400,000 deal would be his reward.

"I'd like to get back on the mountain top with Moses and Doc. I want one of those big contracts like they've got. When I was up there with them, I outplayed all of 'em. How do you think that makes me feel?" Barnes, utilizing an abundance of bogus bluster for emphasis, told *Boston Globe* columnist Bob Ryan. "When I see the million-dollar contracts that they're getting, I get mad at myself because I had the talent to make what they've made over the years. I wasted so many chances that I feel like punching myself. But I love myself too much to do that."

Having stayed clean for more than two months, Barnes made a whole-hearted bid to impress the Nets coaching staff. His efforts paid off as he led the team in both scoring and rebounding and was voted MVP of the summer league. Brown was elated—until New Jersey owner Joe Taub vetoed the plan to sign the free agent because Barnes had skipped out on a mind-boggling $5,000 hotel incidentals tab, forcing the team to cover the charges. Despite the coach's protests, Taub was adamant: there would be no more Bad News.

Once again, Marvin's fondness for self-indulgence had triumphed over common sense.

"I was praying he could prove he wasn't washed up," Brown says. "I knew he came with a lot of baggage, but I thought I could handle him. Back then, I was naïve. I knew nothing about drugs and their effects. I was a young coach who judged players strictly on their talent. If I thought a guy could produce on the court, I wanted him. I begged my owner to give him a second chance, but I was wasting my breath."

Because Barnes had performed so well for the Nets in the summer league, he anticipated there would be contract offers from other NBA teams. There was, however, no interest in his services.

After the summer league had come to an unfortunate conclusion, Barnes moved into his mother's home, with no car, no money, and no job prospects. In the spring of 1982, he was arrested for pimping and pandering, though the charges were eventually dropped. Still, details of the run-in were reported in the local media, as well as in *JET* magazine. Suspecting that the Providence police were tracking his every move, he asked a friend in Watertown, Massachusetts, if he could stay at his house for a month or two.

Even though Barnes knew deep down that his talent had all but evaporated, he could not let go of his love for the game that had long ago offered seemingly unlimited prospects for wealth and fame. He opted to train for a comeback in the Continental Basketball Association (CBA), a minor league system that survived on a shoestring budget by requiring its players to play for dirt-cheap salaries, travel by bus for five or six hours to away games, and stay at trashy hotels or motels.

Attempting to turn back time, Barnes, now thirty, began working out in late August at nearby Boston College, lifting weights and scrimmaging with a number of pros, including

Kevin McHale, Robert Parish, M. L. Carr, and Danny Ainge, as well as members of the school's varsity squad.

It did not take long for reality to sink in.

Usually matched up against McHale, who had been named to the NBA All-Rookie First Team in 1981, Bad News loped along as if he were playing in an over-forty weekend warrior league, sometimes walking off the court mid-play, huffing and puffing while gasping for air. When he did summon up enough energy to guard the Celtics' sixth man, he was subjected to a constant stream of humorous trash talk. "Hey, old timer, you're in my torture chamber now. There's no way out, babe," the twenty-three-year-old future hall of famer joked. "Face it, you're doomed. Take your beating like a man."

If he were in his heyday, the former "spirit of the Spirits," as Barnes had often referred to himself, would have been a worthy opponent for the 6-foot-10 Boston power forward, who possessed the arms of an octopus. Barnes would have been quicker and faster; McHale would have employed his assortment of low-post moves to gain an edge. "You couldn't tell from the games at BC," says Carr, who had been a teammate of both players, "but News, at one time, would have gone right at Kevin because he had no fear. My guess is that Kevin would've come out on top, but watching them go at each other would've been interesting."

After two weeks of being outclassed, Barnes gave up. Walking out of the BC gym for the final time, he tossed a new pair of Converse basketball shoes that McHale had given him into a trash container. He then returned to his friend's home in Watertown to ponder the future.

Failing to see any chance for a career revival, he downed the contents of two nearly full quart bottles of whiskey that he had swiped from his friend's dining room liquor cabinet. By the time his host returned from work that evening, the house reeked of spilled booze and cigarette smoke. All of Barnes's belongings were thrown onto the front lawn, and he was told to "find another sucker to mooch off." The no longer welcome houseguest immediately called Sam, the heroin addict, and asked for a ride to Providence. "And bring along whatever stuff you have."

Five minutes into the trip, Bad News was snorting cocaine.

Basketball and the Spirits called again a month later, but it was a world away from St. Louis and the old ABA. The Detroit Spirits, a new franchise in the CBA, had been trying to get in touch with Barnes through Mama Baxter. She had no details to provide other than the name of a contact and a phone number.

For the previous two weeks, the Providence legend had been making the rounds of his old haunts, hoping to bump into a kindly dealer who would allow him to buy a small quantity of marijuana on credit. The ballers at Bucklin Street Park didn't quite know what to make of the sullen spectator who stood alone 30 feet away from the court, resting his right shoulder against a light pole. A few friends from his high school days came over to greet him, but he was clearly not in the mood for conversation. All he wanted was to score a joint and move on.

Now, after learning about the phone call from Detroit, Barnes sensed an income opportunity. He phoned the team's office and spoke with Sam Washington, the Spirits' general manager, who asked if he would be interested in signing a non-guaranteed contract for $800 a week. During the brief conversation, the former Piston was told he would be the "building block" of the CBA franchise, which was scheduled to start play in a month. "You'll be our highest paid player," the enthusiastic GM told him. "We need someone with your experience to set the tone for our younger guys."

It was an enticing proposal, one Washington would come to regret.

A day after signing, Barnes flew to Detroit and addressed the media at a press conference. "Look at me, all lean and mean. I'm here to show all the young bucks on this team how to play the game," he said, knowing full well his words were nothing more than false bravado. "Don't forget, this is my town. No one can sell tickets here better than News."

Less than three weeks into the season, Barnes suffered a knee sprain, which sidelined him until mid-December. Once the Spirits' "role model" returned to the lineup, he played in only five more games, getting tossed out of two of them, one for fighting and the other for making an obscene gesture at an official. He also missed three practices and one road game because he had slipped badly, having gone on a coke toot with two fellow addicts he had known from his days of tagging along with the Curry Boys.

By late January, Washington could take no more. "I'm tired of sending out search parties every time you pull one of your disappearing acts," the Spirits GM told Barnes. "I don't know why you think you're entitled to do whatever you please. I've got seven young guys busting their butts to make it to the NBA. And then I've got you, a guy who doesn't give a shit. Well, the free ride's over as of today."

Feeling sorry for himself, Bad News cashed his final paycheck and bought $700 worth of cocaine on the same day he was released. A week later, he was out of blow and on his way to a 120-day stint in rehab.

Still not receiving any financial support from Becton, who remained wary of the feds bringing charges against him, Barnes took another stab at reviving his career by signing with the Ohio Mixers of the CBA in November of 1983.

As had been the case with many of his previous teams, he was not the only player on the roster who was considerably off-kilter. "We brought in three high-salaried ex-NBA players—Marvin,

Kevin Williams, and Billy Ray Bates—and all of them had major issues," former Mixers head coach Tom Sawyer says. "Every day was bedlam."

"Between Billy Ray, Kevin and me, I was the sane one," Barnes said. "Trust me on that."

Only twenty-two years old, Williams had been the '83 second-round draft choice of the Spurs. The talented 6-foot-2 point guard had earned a spot on San Antonio's roster but lasted only 19 games due solely to his violent and uncontrollable temper, which resulted in frequent brawls with opponents and teammates alike. "Kevin took things a little too personal on the court," Barnes said, "but no one had more heart, which is why he ended up playing in the NBA for a few [actually four] more years."

Bates, the leading scorer for the Portland Trail Blazers in both the 1980 and '81 playoffs, had become an incorrigible alcoholic and drug abuser by the time he was waived out of the NBA and signed by the Mixers. "He didn't stay too long, maybe a month or two. Then he went to play in the Philippines for a lot more money," Barnes said. "The man loved to drink. Even had a beer gut. But hear me: Billy Ray could show up for a game totally pie-eyed and still score 30."[1]

And then, of course, the Mixers' coach had his hands full keeping tabs on Barnes.

"Marvin's idea of practicing was to stand around and tell stories about the good old days," Sawyer says. "When we would start our running drills, he'd go up and down the court a few times and then disappear into the locker room. Our staff would watch him sneak out. Then we'd start laughing about how he thought he was

---

1 In 1998, Bates, totally soused, robbed a gas station attendant at knifepoint in New Jersey and fled with only $7. He was arrested less than an hour later and eventually served five years in Bayside State Prison.

tricking us. The simple truth was that he just couldn't keep up with our younger guys.

"We had all these big-name players, and we still were only a .500 club. After a while, fans stopped coming to our games. Somehow we ended up making the playoffs, but we didn't get past the first round."

After playing a handful of games for another CBA team, the Evansville Thunder, in 1984, Barnes unceremoniously walked away from the game. "I had gone from ABA Rookie of the Year, to the NBA, to Italy, to the CBA, to the unemployment line in less than ten years. Somewhere along the way I had lost every ounce of pride. I was a 'has-been' at age thirty-two."

Eighteen

CALIFORNIA DREAMIN'

It was no coincidence that less than a year before Barnes retired from the game, the NBA adopted the first comprehensive anti-drug policy in pro sports, with testing specifically designed to punish players who were using cocaine and/or heroin. By then, numerous accounts of Bad News's outlandish behavior due to substance abuse had long been circulating around the league.

"Hey, I'm the reason why the NBA took such a hard-line stand against drug use in '83," Barnes once said, sounding very much as if he were boasting.

Yet he was hardly the only well-known player who became addicted during the seventies and early eighties. Perennial NBA All-Stars David Thompson, George Gervin, and Walter Davis all were cocaine abusers at some point during their careers, but they, for the most part, were able to mask their dependencies. Others, including Bernard King, battled to overcome alcoholism.

"Barnes's pattern of conduct was definitely a factor in why we were anxious to see a tough anti-drug policy established," said Charles Grantham, former executive director of the NBA Players Association. "His name came up a number of times during discussions about how drug use was giving the league and us a black eye. Our members were fed up reading newspaper articles about guys who had been caught using illegal substances. Players who had always been clean didn't want fans thinking the NBA was becoming a league of addicts. That's why we overwhelmingly voted for the 'three strikes and you're out' penalty."

The historic agreement, which offered help to those players who sought it while also serving as a deterrent for those who might be tempted to use, came seven years too late for Barnes. By the time the policy took effect, he was an unsympathetic sponger with no apparent purpose in life, a ridiculed flimflam artist who relied upon the generosity of friends and strangers alike to carry on one day at a time.

There was a simple explanation why the penniless schemer had not asked Becton for a handout in more than two years. The long arm of the law had reached out for the drug trafficker and his associates in late 1981 after Hindelang was caught red-handed in a St. Louis warehouse that was filled to the ceiling with eight and a half tons of marijuana.

"I walked into the building and started feeling lightheaded just from breathing in the air," says US Attorney Mike Reap. "We took samples from each bale of pot for evidence, shot video of the contraband, and then hauled all 17,000 pounds of the stuff to an incinerator and burned it. We had Hindelang cold, and he was angling for a deal. It was an easy sell to get him to cooperate with our investigation."

Serving as a government snitch, the mobster who had master-minded the offshore pot smuggling enterprise was permitted by law enforcement officials to maintain an active role in the deal-ings of the organization.

Based principally upon detailed verbal and written reports supplied by Hindelang and another high-ranking member of the drug ring whose name has never been made public, Reap charged Becton with participating in a continuing criminal enterprise, two interstate drug charges, and a misdemeanor charge of possession of cocaine. At trial, Hindelang testified that he had sold between three and four million dollars' worth of marijuana to Becton between 1976 and 1980.

The prosecution stated that, on at least two occasions, Becton traveled to Florida from St. Louis, rented a house, and supervised the distribution of more than 7,000 pounds of pot to various buyers across the country.

As a result of his leadership role in the marijuana trafficking operations, Becton was convicted and sentenced to twenty-five years in prison, of which he served seventeen. He was also fined $50,000. "I'll say this for the guy, he had a lot of friends in high places," Reap says. "He persuaded a congressman to petition the judge for leniency, and practically the entire St. Louis city council appeared as character witnesses at his sentencing hearing."

Despite his longtime involvement in drug smuggling, Hindelang received an extremely light punishment. "In the end, it amounted to nothing more than a slap on the wrist," one DEA agent says. "When he received only ten years, I was upset. When he ended up serving just thirty months, I was fuming. The man was a snake, and unfortunately he was rewarded for being one."

As for Barnes, he was of little interest to the feds. "We knew all about him," an undercover investigator says, "but he was a small fish, someone who was along the ride. We wanted the top four or five guys in the organization, the people who were running the show. We weren't about to waste our time trying to go after some washed-up jock."

Although Hindelang claimed his cash assets were only $694,000 at the time of his arrest, two relentless members of law enforcement, Chuck Visco of the Monroe County's sheriff's office in Florida and an undercover female ICE agent, decided to take a closer look at his finances.

During the course of what was codenamed "Operation Cash Extraction," it was uncovered that Big Ed and his relatives were linked to eighty-six shell corporations, mainly based in Panama and Costa Rica. In addition, an extensive piece-by-piece document search proved there were also direct connections to ownership of a condo and two houses in Aspen, ranches in Montana and Oregon, forty-three oil wells in Pennsylvania; as well as bank accounts and trusts in Switzerland, England, Lichtenstein, the Isle of Mann, Jersey, and Guernsey.

The outcome of the probe: Hindelang agreed to forfeit $50 million to the government.

Were all of his ill-gotten gains recovered? "We're still actively looking," Visco says. "I can tell you for sure that Hindelang isn't in the poor house, and no one in law enforcement is shedding any tears for the guy. He drives around in a new $50,000 car and lives in a Santa Barbara, California, home that has to be worth a couple million bucks. Draw your own conclusions about how he manages to maintain such a lavish lifestyle."

With Becton unable to provide any financial aid, Barnes moved back to Detroit in March of 1985, where he panhandled, ate an occasional meal at a soup kitchen, and usually slept in a homeless shelter.

When an NBA club would arrive in town for a game against the Pistons, Barnes would show up at the visiting team's hotel and wait in the lobby for the players to walk by. Looking unkempt and usually wearing a threadbare sweat suit, he'd ask those he knew from his playing days if they could "loan" him a hundred dollars. Out of pity, most reached into their wallets and gave him enough money to buy a few decent meals.

One day Barnes stopped by Mama Baxter's place. He was greeted by a very eager Baxter, who informed Marvin that Bill Walton had phoned for him.

When Barnes returned the call, the Clippers center asked for his help. It seemed Walton had been given permission to negotiate his own trade, and the Celtics had expressed an interest in acquiring him. If a deal could be arranged, the thirty-three-year-old would have what might be his last opportunity to win a second NBA championship in the role of sixth man on a team that had Larry Bird, Robert Parish, Kevin McHale, Dennis Johnson, and Danny Ainge in its starting lineup.

Barnes was asked to fly out to San Diego, stay at Walton's home, and help him get into game shape for the 1985–86 season. Hours after the conversation, Marvin and his new girlfriend, Valerie, packed what little baggage they had and boarded a jet for balmy Southern California.

Walton could have asked any one of his teammates or any number of other pros who lived in the San Diego area to train with him. Instead, he had gone to great lengths to contact Barnes, who hadn't played pro ball in almost three years. "The one thing I always knew about Marvin was that he was a ferocious competitor," the Hall of Fame center says. "It didn't matter that I was four inches taller and 25 pounds heavier. He was going to battle me for every rebound and contest every shot I took. Maybe his skills weren't what they used to be, but I needed someone who wouldn't back down, someone who'd push me. He was the only guy I could count on to get me to where I wanted to be."

Barnes later would flatter himself by stating, "A thoroughbred needs to work out with another thoroughbred. A thoroughbred don't race against no plow horse."

The .7-acre Walton estate, located in the Marston Hills section of San Diego, was a sports-oriented paradise designed for both kids and kids at heart.

The bi-level 6,300-square-foot house, aptly named "California Dreamin'," was built in Spanish Revival style and contained sixteen rooms, including six bedrooms, two of which were decorated with posters, album covers, T-shirts, and other mementos that paid homage to music legends Bob Dylan and Neil Young.

Just off the front door hallway was a game room that featured a pool table, a 14-foot-long fully stocked bar, and four display cases that held trophies, plaques, medals, and championship game balls.

The living room was the most traditionally styled area of the house, a relatively quiet place filled with treasured family pictures and keepsakes. Built into a wall were two floor-to-ceiling seven-foot wide bookcases that were crammed with works about politics, history, law, and sports.

Throughout the home, souvenirs of Walton's many adventures with his favorite band, the Grateful Dead, were prominently displayed. On a few of the downstairs walls were classic photographs that captured highlights of the diehard Deadhead's remarkable basketball career, as well as certificates and plaques he had received for his many charitable endeavors.

Overlooking one of Balboa Park's most scenic canyons and no more than a stone's throw away from the San Diego Zoo, the private compound was built for relaxation and recreation. Leading out to the family's pool and hot tub was a winding slate path lined with exotic plants and swaying tropical trees. A three-car garage had been converted into a weight room, complete with a ping pong table, working bar, and lounge area that showcased a monstrous drum set given to Walton by Grateful Dead percussionist Mickey Hart. Off the side patio was, of course, a basketball court. A tennis court and a two-bedroom guesthouse were tucked away 40 yards down a sloped trail that led from the side door of the family home.

Walton had a well-deserved reputation of throwing wild parties at California Dreamin' during the summer, but once the two-a-day training sessions with Barnes began, he put a temporary halt to all the nighttime revelry.

"From the moment I arrived, Bill was all business," Barnes said. "Before I even unpacked my suitcase, he handed me a four-page handwritten workout schedule. I read though it and thought, 'Damn, he's out to kill us both.'"

Their routine began each day at 8 a.m. with 15 minutes of calisthenics, followed by two hours of shooting and rebounding drills. After lunch, they headed back to the basketball court for another 90 minutes of intense one-on-one competition, followed by a half hour of weightlifting. To cool down, the pair always finished with a one-mile jog through the upscale neighborhood.

In the evenings while Walton went for a ten-mile bike ride, Barnes cruised around town in his host's vintage wood-paneled station wagon, listened to music, or enjoyed a soothing whirlpool. His favorite pastime, though, was roughhousing with Walton's sons, Adam, Nathan, Luke (named after Maurice Lucas), and Chris, who ranged in age from three to eight. The kids had so much fun with their new playmate that they started calling him "Uncle Marvin." Bill's wife, Susie, however, was not at all pleased with the family's rambunctious houseguest because she believed he was encouraging her boys to fight and allowing them to watch violent TV shows. When she scolded the children for wrestling in the house, they would yell back, "But, mom, Uncle Marvin gave us permission." Needless to say, that answer did not sit well with her.

After two months of heavy training and uneasy waiting, Walton received the phone call that revitalized his career. It was from Celtics President and General Manager Red Auerbach, who informed the 1978 league MVP that Boston had acquired him in exchange for veteran forward Cedric Maxwell, a first-round draft choice, and cash. Auerbach said he was gambling that Walton, despite chronic foot and back problems, could play 15 to 20 minutes a game as a backup to both Parish at center and McHale at power forward.

When Walton, who, due to injuries, had played in only a total of 169 games from 1978 through 1985, inquired when he would be required to take a physical, Auerbach replied, "Don't worry about it. We both know you have no shot of passing it."

After thanking his new boss profusely, Walton hung up the phone and started celebrating by breaking into an Indian war dance. "It's a done deal, brother. I'm officially a Celtic," he told Marvin. "Why don't you come to Boston with me? I'll talk Red into giving you a contract. You, me, Bird, McHale, and Parish. Now that's what I call an All-Star frontcourt. Who could stop us?"

The suggestion, of course, was preposterous. "Forget that, Bill," Barnes said. "Let me put it this way: If you even mentioned my name to Auerbach, he'd send you straight back here on the first plane out of Logan [Airport]."

A day later, Barnes decided to move on. "We both know damn well that Susie wanted to kick my ass to the curb weeks ago," he told his friend. "Now that you're all set with Boston, my job's done here."

Walton immediately called the San Diego Marriott on West Harbor Drive and paid in advance for Marvin and Valerie to enjoy a week's stay. He also handed his workout partner $1,000 in cash. "Figure out what you want to do, and then let me know," he said. "I'll help you any way I can." It was a generous gesture, but Barnes had already formulated a short-term plan. He'd use most of the money he had just received to buy a two-week supply of coke and weed.

Relaxing at a first-class hotel was enjoyable while it lasted, but by the time Marvin and Valerie checked out, their funds were down to less than $50. They would have to survive by living on the streets.

It might seem like there are far worse places than Southern California to be homeless. After all, the region is known for its pleasant climate, beautifully landscaped residential communities, pristine beaches, and modern business complexes. But in City Heights, the oozing cesspool of East San Diego where the couple ended up, there weren't any pretty-as-a-picture-postcard tourist attractions. For six days, they stayed in an overcrowded, foul-smelling shelter until Valerie got drunk and started a lengthy shouting war with Marvin, forcing the manager to evict them. Moments later, the pair parted ways for good.

With dope dominating his life, Barnes paid little attention to nutrition as he wandered the ghetto without purpose. Occasionally he'd stand on a long food line at a mission to get a bowl of cereal and two pieces of toast for breakfast. Around lunchtime, he might take a few bites of a ham and cheese sandwich before throwing the rest away. By 5 p.m., he'd again be seeking to satisfy his hunger—not for a decent meal but for drugs of any kind.

Embarrassed by the life choices he had made and terrified of what the future might hold, Barnes vegetated in squalor for more than fourteen months. At night, the once-proud athlete slept underneath an Escondido Freeway bridge or in a thickly wooded park, which provided a small degree of shelter in case of rain. If the weather turned cold, he would seek refuge in a basement laundry room of an apartment building.

When he managed to bum a few dollars from sympathetic strangers, some of whom recognized him from his brief time with the Clippers, he would pay for a room at a $6-a-night flophouse where he could brush his teeth, shower, and shave. Every so often he'd take a bus to Marston Hills and wait until after midnight to sneak onto Walton's property, where he would catch a few hours' sleep on a couch in the weight room after raiding a mini-refrigerator for beer and cold cuts. "I could have just knocked on Bill and Susie's front door," he said, "but I didn't want anyone inside to see me looking like a damn hobo."

While crashing in a crack house one night, Barnes awoke to discover that his carryall containing clothes and two pairs of basketball shoes had been stolen. All he had left was what he was wearing: a grubby Detroit Spirits T-shirt and gym shorts. For two weeks he went barefoot, with a filthy ripped orange blanket thrown over his shoulders. Finally, he placed a collect call to his mother, who sent a FedEx package containing a Providence College sweat suit, T-shirts, underwear, gym shorts, white socks, and a pair of sneakers.

For a while he lived in a fire-ravaged house that had no roof. At night he would lay awake, staring into the sky while lying on a grimy, mold-covered mattress as rats scurried back and forth across the charred floor. His only companions were seven illegal immigrants from Mexico, none of whom spoke a word of English. They always offered to share their food, but Barnes had no appetite. "I looked like one of those starving African children you see in the UNICEF commercials on TV. I lost so much weight that my shorts kept sliding down to my ankles."

Even though Lula or one of his friends back home, most often Kevin Stacom, would occasionally wire him a few hundred dollars for food and clothing, he'd instead spend most—if not all—of the money on coke and booze.

"I knew that some of the cash I wired to him had to be going for drugs," Stacom says, "but Marvin needed money to eat, and I wasn't about to let him starve to death."

Barnes's solitary existence beat the alternative of being an inviting mark out in the open of what East San Diego County sheriffs described as the most dangerous urban war zone in America. "Gang members, drug dealers, just plain street hustlers, they'd shoot people for no reason," he once said. "Unless you knew an out-of-the-way hiding spot, there was no such thing as a safe place to bed down at night."

One afternoon while in a stupor, Barnes met an attractive twenty-six-year-old cocaine addict named Alice. When asked what she wanted to do with her life, she said her goal was to become a successful hooker. Keenly aware of the nightly dangers she would face while soliciting business on the streets, Marvin attempted to dissuade her from pursuing such a perilous line of work. Alice, however, had no reservations.

"If you're sure that's what you want to do, I'll try to look after you," Barnes said. "Understand, whether I'm close by or not, trouble's bound to come your way."

To further Alice's career, he became her "chilly pimp," street lingo for a man who manages a single prostitute. As things turned out, she quickly learned how to attract "johns" who paid well and treated her decently. In a typical week, she made $700 turning tricks, which was financially rewarding for Barnes, whose only source of income was the money she gave him for being her guardian.

After managing to stay safe in East San Diego's no man's land for more than four years, Barnes wound up behind bars in August of 1989 after being arrested for shoplifting lingerie and nine movies from an X-rated video store. Because he had been convicted of a misdemeanor burglary earlier in the year, the thirty-six-year-old vagrant was charged with two felony counts of petty theft. Taken downtown and booked, he was held for trial at the county detention center, where inmates were treated as if they were cattle.

While Barnes was locked up, Providence College officials discovered he was only three credits shy of graduating. The school, eager to see one of its legendary athletes obtain a diploma, offered him the opportunity to write an eight-page book report on author Joseph Wambaugh's police novel, *The New Centurions*, which would complete his degree requirements.

Laboring to complete the paper, Barnes placed a call to Bill Reynolds at the *Providence Journal*, told him about his final college assignment, and sought some advice.

"As one writer to another," Barnes said, "tell me what you do when you've written all you have, and it's not long enough."

"How many pages have you done?" Reynolds asked.

"Two," Marvin replied. "Then I ran out of things to say."

In record time, he had developed a severe case of writer's block. Creating six additional pages eventually proved to be too much of a challenge, so he shelved the project and passed up the chance to graduate.

At his next court appearance, Barnes was sentenced to sixteen months at the R. J. Donovan Correctional Facility in San

Diego. The prison was Club Med compared to ACI in Rhode Island, where he had been incarcerated a decade earlier. All the inmates in his cellblock were at least thirty years old and classified as non-violent offenders—illegal immigrants, drug users, petty thieves, and white-collar criminals. Serving time there was actually somewhat relaxing for the weary nomad. He could read, exercise, watch TV, chow down on three hot meals a day, and, although not by choice, regain his sobriety.

Paroled after six months, Barnes was transferred to a state-run transitional residence. During his first two months there, he re-read Wambaugh's work, organized his thoughts, and composed a thirteen-page book report for school. Receiving a passing grade, he was now officially a college grad. "It took me sixteen years, but I finally got things right."

Released from the halfway house in July of 1990, Marvin returned to the dregs of City Heights where he reunited with Alice, who was still working the street corners, trolling for customers.

A local reporter, hoping to interview the former Clipper about his recent misfortunes, tracked him down as he was panhandling outside the East County Pawn Shop. Barnes, thinking he had struck gold when the journalist attempted to question him about his run of bad luck, told the young man, "You give me a thousand dollars, and I'll tell you things that will make you famous. I've got stories that'll make headlines. No sugarcoating. I mean I'll name names for you. If you deal with me, you're in the big leagues, partner. I'll be talking about gangsters, bank robbers, Colombian drug traffickers, homosexual athletes, prison murders and rapes,

Nineteen

BEHIND PRISON WALLS

Soon after Lula Barnes had read Reynolds's two-part feature article about her son's misadventures in paradise in the *Providence Journal*, she asked one of his ex-girlfriends, Donna Johnson, to travel to San Diego and save him from becoming a "hood rat."

Problem was that Marvin had no desire to be rescued.

"I'm pretty sure his mother had to bribe him just to get him to meet with me," Donna says. "As soon as I spotted Marvin, I could tell how much he was hurting. He had sunken eyes and a blank stare. The skin on his face and hands was all cracked and shriveled up."

All Barnes wanted was to be left alone, but Donna had other ideas. "I'm going be doggin' you until you agree to go back to Providence with me," she told him. "You're destroying yourself here. You're wasting away to nothing. Just look in a mirror." Staying by his side for two weeks and practically resorting to force-feeding him, she finally coaxed him into accompanying her to Rhode Island, where he received medical attention and drug therapy.

In December of 1991, Barnes, who was still on probation for his minor brush with the law in California, accepted a part-time job offer from Rhode Island's then–attorney general, James

O'Neil, who asked him to speak to groups of inner-city teenagers. Despite the fact that he seemed to be doing well in his new position, Barnes could not fight off his urges to use again. As soon as Lula learned that her son was on the prowl, she went before the state parole board. "Either you get my boy help, or I'm going to the newspapers," she said. "He needs care, not punishment."

Aware of the anguish he was causing his mother, Barnes called Grantham at the NBA Players Association to seek information about where to receive long-term counseling. He was advised to contact the John Lucas Treatment Center, a rehab facility in Houston run by the ex-pro point guard and the same place Gerard had managed to kick his habit in 1990.

"I knew John's whole deal about being a dope fiend back in his playing days," Barnes said. "There was one story going around that his teammates had taped a sign on the back of his warm-up jacket that said, 'Things go better with coke.' I remembered reading about him wandering through the ghetto in a three-piece suit, wearing four pairs of sweat socks and not having shoes on his feet. Some cops found him in an alley, all beat up, out of his mind, high as a kite. I was sure someone like him could understand my situation. A day after the two of us talked, I was on a plane to Houston."

Suffering from the "shakes" and malnutrition, Barnes began treatment as a patient on a locked-down ward at Gulf Pines Hospital. After five days of detox, he was transferred to the rehab facility. Still disoriented, he was cautioned that the odds were stacked against him. "I'm going to tell you what you need to hear, not what you want to hear," Lucas told him. "First of all, admit that you need help. Then be smart enough to realize that beating your habit is going to be a lifelong struggle. It never gets easy. Give in just once to temptation, and you'll probably never get sober again. I've known guys like that, and you'll be one of them unless you fight your disease every minute of every day.

"Bottom line, the brain loves that harmless-looking snowy white powder. The drug has my utmost respect. It's patient. It's always there waiting for me to make a mistake."

Barnes did so well while undergoing ninety days of in-patient care that Grantham, after consulting with Lucas, offered him employment. The Players Association was seeking a former member who had overcome addiction to speak to NBA teams about his experiences and to explain in graphic terms the toll drugs can take on a player's career and personal life. The job, Barnes was told, would begin in ten months, in time for the start of the 1993 training camps. "We think you're a perfect fit because of all you've been through, including losing millions of dollars, living on the streets, and serving time in prison," Grantham explained. "You can communicate with players far better than some professional counselor who has never touched a basketball. You can warn these young men about all the temptations they're going to face sooner or later. This is your chance to have an impact on their futures. You can help these guys simply by being truthful about your experiences."

Without even inquiring what his salary would be, Barnes accepted the position.

Upon completing the treatment program, he was appointed house manager at the rehab center. His principal duties were to counsel suspended NBA players Roy Tarpley and Richard Dumas, along with four other addicts. As a gesture of good faith, Lucas permitted his new employee to live in an off-site apartment at night and supervise the patients at the facility during the day. "I felt real good about myself and the work I was doing. Plus, I had a great job all lined up with the Players Association."

His first out-of-town assignment came several weeks after Tarpley, who had won the NBA's Sixth Man of the Year Award as a member of the Dallas Mavs in 1988, had finished his rehab stay. Banned indefinitely from playing in the league, the power forward had begun a comeback attempt with the Wichita Falls Texans, a CBA team. Despite having been given the opportunity to redeem himself, the twenty-six-year-old was on the verge of relapsing.

"Talked to Roy this morning. Sounds like he's climbing the walls," Lucas told Barnes. "He'll be looking to make a buy within a day or two if he doesn't get support. I want you to catch the next plane to Wichita Falls. Once you get there, room with him. Babysit him. Don't let him out of your sight. Keep him focused. Take as much time as you need. This man's on the edge, but he probably doesn't realize it."

Barnes drove to his apartment, packed a suitcase, and drove to the airport. By just a few minutes, he missed his flight, the only one scheduled to Wichita Falls that day. Knowing that so much trust had been placed on him, he became distraught that he had botched his first major mission. Rather than contacting Lucas at once, he drove to a strip club near the airport, where he calmed his frayed nerves by guzzling three shots of bourbon. Those few shooters were all it took to set him off on a full-blown drug spree. Less than three hours later, he was snorting cocaine. Gone was his job as house manager. Gone was the prospect of counseling NBA players. Now his only ambition was to get blasted as often as possible.

"There are those who can't be saved," Lucas would later explain to a reporter. "They might be looking for help, but their resolve isn't just weak, it's non-existent. It boils down to this: Their need to use drugs is more urgent than their desire to stay clean. Marvin may just be one of those guys who never gets sober even though he's aware that he is slowly but surely destroying himself. All he had to do was call me and I would have rebooked his flight reservation for the next day. He should have been able to figure out what the right thing to do was, but addicts don't think rationally. They panic."

When Donna, who was staying with Barnes in Houston, found out what he had done, she told him point blank: "The problem is that you're afraid to succeed. It's that simple. Without drugs in your system, you're insecure and frightened. That's a shame, too, because you're a grown man."

Her words, true as they were, had no impact.

A month later, Barnes was in the process of selling ten grams of cocaine to an acquaintance when three cops, guns drawn, jumped out of an unmarked white van and placed him under arrest. Charged with delivery of a controlled substance, he was subsequently found guilty and sentenced to six years at Lynaugh State Prison in Fort Stockton, Texas. At the same time as he was incarcerated, his sister was locked up in a federal penitentiary, finishing a ten-year stretch for possession of 72 grams of crack.

It was the fourth time Bad News had been imprisoned (the fifth, counting his four-day confinement in an Italian dungeon). He soon found out that Lynaugh, technically classified as a medium-security facility, was strictly dog-eat-dog, where inmates fought for their lives while guards placed wagers on who would prevail in the savage skirmishes. Only when a combatant was knocked out or killed did the correctional officers step in to view the casualty of prison warfare, staring down at the defeated gladiator lying motionless on a cement floor covered by a pool of fresh blood. "The guards here don't break up fights," Barnes told *Houston Chronicle* reporter Michael Murphy. "They pick up bodies."

Having learned from past prison experiences how to become "everybody's friend," Barnes earned special privileges for good behavior after serving less than a year of his sentence. He was also given the undemanding job of supervising the inmates' basketball league. As part of his responsibilities, he went from one cellblock to the next, signing up those convicts who wanted to compete. If, however, a prisoner's name wasn't on the list supplied to him by the assistant warden, it meant the individual was not allowed to participate because he had violated one of the many strict rules of the institution.

While recruiting prospective players, he came face to face with a 6-foot-2, 250-pound battle-scarred lifer nicknamed "Hammerhead."

"Hey, I want in. Put me on a team," the man, who was all sleeved up with tattoos on both arms, demanded. Barnes checked the list, but the inmate's name was not on the roster of eligible participants. "Can't help you, partner," he said. "You must've done something wrong."

Agitated and clearly unstable, the inmate crouched into a wrestler's stance, preparing to attack. Well aware of the man's reputation as a brawler, Barnes called out to one of the guards, who was standing no more than 15 feet away. "Hey, boss, keep him away from me," he pleaded. "The man's gone mental. Don't want no trouble here."

Instead of attempting to restrain the incensed prisoner, the jailer retreated to his glass-enclosed sentry station, looking on as Barnes backpedaled.

"Understand, I wasn't afraid of the guy. I'd been lifting weights in the prison yard every day. I was a solid 220, easy," said Barnes. "No one in Lynaugh had ever fucked with me until then." What did concern Barnes was that he was scheduled to speak to a group of students at a local high school the following day and, if he were forced to defend himself, it might well jeopardize his chance to gain a taste of freedom.

"It might not sound like much," he later told a reporter, "but if you were stuck in an eight-by-ten cell for fourteen hours a day, you would do anything to be on the outside, even for a short time."

Without the guard's intervention, Barnes would have no choice but to take on the demented prisoner. "This man ain't all there. Do something, please," he again shouted to the officer.

"He's your problem, not mine" the guard answered.

In one last bid to avoid a fight, Barnes raised his arms above his head. The pacifying gesture was totally futile. Seconds later, he ducked a punch and retaliated, landing two quick jabs and an uppercut, none of which slowed his attacker. Finally, a solid hook sent Hammerhead staggering backward onto the concrete.

"I turned my back on him and started walking away. I thought for sure the man had to be out cold," Barnes said, "but somehow he got back up and tackled me from behind. Now I was the one who turned animal. I flipped him on his back, got on top of him, and started wailing away. No bullshit, I wanted to put an end to this brother's miserable life. Must have banged his head on the concrete damn near fifteen times, even though I knew, at some point, he had to be unconscious. The only reason I finally stopped was because my arms were too sore to keep going."

It took the guard several minutes to revive the severely beaten inmate and help him to his feet. Then the two exhausted enemies were put in shackles and brought before the warden, who wanted to know why Barnes showed no signs of being in a fight while the other man's head was matted with blood. "This sucker wanted to destroy me, to put me out of commission for good," the prison's basketball coordinator said. "If I hadn't knocked him out, he would have kept on trying to kill me."

Because the guard verified the account, Barnes did not get written up. He was even allowed to speak at the local high school the next day. As part of his talk, he recounted every detail of his life-or-death battle with his fellow convict as an example of how inhuman prison life can be.

With only six months remaining until his parole date, Barnes jeopardized his chances for early release by becoming romantically involved with a female guard named Carol. Every day she brought him gifts, including snacks, money for the commissary, and cologne. For 15 minutes each afternoon, the two had sex in an air-conditioned trailer, which was normally used by the guards to relax when they took their cigarette and coffee breaks. The smitten couple also exchanged passionate love letters on a daily basis.

However, a serious problem arose when one of Barnes's intimate messages fell out of Carol's uniform as it was being put into a washer in the prison laundry room. The two-page note was retrieved by a civilian employee and turned over to an administrator. If it could be proven that the pair was involved in a sexual relationship, she would immediately be fired and he would have an extra year tacked onto his sentence.

Summoned to the warden's office, he was shown the steamy evidence. "This ain't mine," Barnes swore while skimming through the letter. "Never seen it before."

"Well, I compared it to your handwriting," the warden replied, "and I'd be willing to bet it's yours. I've warned the guard, and now I'm warning you. Stay away from each other."

Even though there was no conclusive proof of a violation, Barnes was placed in solitary confinement for a week. When he was released on probation in late 1995 after serving two years and nine months, he moved in with Carol, who by then had quit her job at the prison.

The relationship abruptly soured three months later. "We were arguing every day. I wanted out, but it wasn't going to be easy. One night after one of our knock-down-drag-outs, I found Carol in the bedroom, holding a gun. When I asked what she was doing, she told me, 'I can't live like this. I've got two bullets in the chamber, one for each of us.' I calmed her down and wrestled the gun away from her. Our affair had turned into a case of fatal attraction. She wasn't about to let me just walk out of her life. I knew I had to come up with a plan which would make *her* want to get rid of *me*."

He decided that the surest way to make her angry enough to throw him out was to go on a nonstop cocaine binge. "For a week, I got high, right in the apartment, right in front of her," he said. "When I told her I thought she'd be better off without me, she agreed with me and even helped pack my bags."

Barnes soon reunited with Donna, the girlfriend who had prodded him into leaving the slums of San Diego in 1990. The couple, along with Donna's twelve-year-old son, Mel, moved into an apartment in Houston. However, they soon began to experience financial problems, which forced them to face the possibility of being evicted. Marvin, however, crafted a bailout solution. He called the Players Association and asked whether he could receive a lump-sum settlement on his NBA pension, which wouldn't kick in until 2002. He was told that he qualified for an immediate one-time payment of approximately $60,000. When he conferred with Grantham, who by then had resigned as director of the union, he was urged not to accept the deal. "If you turn it down, you'll get at least $30,000 a year for life once you turn fifty. My advice is to be patient and wait until you're eligible to receive your full pension."

In Barnes's tunnel-vision view, however, the lump-sum package would enable the thirty-eight-year-old to pay off all his debts, make a few necessary purchases, and provide himself with a decent financial cushion in case of an unexpected emergency. After all, he thought, odds were he'd probably be dead and gone before his fiftieth birthday. So he signed on the dotted line, cashed his settlement check, and relinquished all retirement benefits.

He used $6,000 to pay off bills, bought a new car for Donna, who would become his wife in January of 1996; spent $15,000 on clothes, furniture, and appliances; and deposited $19,000 in the couple's bank account. Clean and sober, Marvin was certain he had made a prudent decision.

But, eight months after receiving his check, he fell off the wagon, which led to him squandering every last dollar remaining from the windfall. "When I started using again, I headed straight to bum's row. Every city's got one. I didn't want to hear Donna nagging at me to get professional help. Addicts, especially me, just want to be by themselves. They want to be free to make a buy here and there without any hassles. That's just what I did in Houston, getting lost and staying lost for about two weeks. Then, for no reason other than running out of cash, I came home."

It seemed nothing would ever permanently curb his voracious appetite for drugs.

The 1986 death of twenty-two-year-old Celtics' first-round draft choice Len Bias in a University of Maryland dorm room due to heart failure caused by cocaine intoxication hadn't been a deterrent, and neither had the 1993 tragic passing of Boston All-Star guard Reggie Lewis, who suffered a fatal seizure while casually practicing his free throw shooting at Brandeis University. In clinical terms, the twenty-seven-year-old died due to hypertrophic cardiomyopathy, an abnormal thickening of the heart muscles. However, Dr. Gilbert Mudge, a cardiologist who had originally misdiagnosed the ailment as nothing more than a fainting disorder, would claim in a court case that two weeks before Lewis's death, the affable athlete, who was widely admired for his work in the community, had privately admitted to him that he had recently been using cocaine.

"I had seen the reports on ESPN and read in the newspapers about how both of them had died," Barnes said. "I thought to myself, 'That couldn't happen to me. Their deaths were just freak accidents.'"

In December of 1996, the forty-four-year-old Barnes, who had just completed a 30-day rehab program, landed a counselor's position at the Golden Eagle Leadership Academy in Houston. According to its brochure, the institution was a strictly regimented substance abuse treatment program for males between the ages of thirteen and seventeen. The instructors at the thirty-bed facility, which was funded by the State of Texas, emphasized "military-style discipline and individual responsibility." In other words, the academy was a glorified boot camp, one embroiled in constant controversy.

Golden Eagle's program director was a black militant leader named Quanell X, a former drug dealer from the Sunnyside section of Houston and a follower of extremist Nation of Islam leader Louis Farrakhan. Oftentimes, Quanell X was portrayed in the media as a hatemonger and a rabble-rouser. In a televised speech to the black community in Houston, Quanell X said, "If you feel you have to mug somebody because of your hurt and pain, go to River Oaks and mug you some good white folks. . . . Give these white folks hell from the womb to the tomb." He later apologized for his racial outburst, but there were many outraged area residents who doubted his sincerity.

There were also allegations that Quanell X and his all-black staff were using their authority at Golden Eagle to indoctrinate the teenage African American residents in the beliefs of the Nation of Islam.

Barnes, though, distanced himself from the program director's incendiary remarks. "I was there to help the kids turn their lives around, no other reason," he would later say. "I wasn't into politics and protests. I was trying to get through to the kids by telling them about the mistakes I'd made. My one and only message: If you keep on making all the wrong choices, you're going to end up either being in prison for life or becoming a murder statistic."

A former ABA executive called Barnes at work one day to invite him to the league's thirtieth anniversary reunion, which was to be held in Indianapolis in August of 1997. It would be a chance for him to share memories of his glory days with many ex-St. Louis teammates, as well as stars from opposition teams. More importantly, the occasion would allow him to rekindle his friendship with former Spirits owner Ozzie Silna, whom he hadn't seen or talked to in twenty years.

The textile tycoon obviously had some legitimate reasons to blame Barnes to a small degree for his team's demise. Still, the one-time rebel without a cause believed Silna would be in a forgiving mood. Deep down, he knew the man whom he had fondly called "Pops" still had a tender spot for him despite all his irresponsible acts as a young player. The assessment proved to be correct.

Once Barnes arrived at the three-day celebration, his first call was to Silna, who posed a few questions to begin their conversation. "I've heard all about your problems, Marvin. Be honest with me. Are you doing all right? Do you need anything? I want to help if I can. Let's meet downstairs in an hour for dinner and we'll talk." For the rest of the weekend, Barnes ate every meal and attended every function with Ozzie and his brother, Danny, former Spirits counsel Donald Schupak, and their wives.

"Whatever you decide to do with the rest of your life, I want to be involved," Ozzie, who was well known for his many philanthropic deeds, told Marvin privately. "I should have gotten in touch with you a long time ago. That was my mistake. Now I want to mentor you, keep you focused, and make sure you're heading in the right direction. Just the fact that you're here and off the drugs tells me all I need to know. I want to see you become a success story. I hope you understand that can still happen for you."

At the reunion's grand banquet, Barnes, despite having played only two seasons in the ABA, was named—along with twenty-nine others—to the league's All-Time Team. Before the awards presentation, he and Costas performed a skit at the podium. With a straight face, the NBC broadcaster mentioned he had been trying to get in touch with his old friend for years but didn't know how to contact him. "Come on, Bob," replied Bad News, with a fake touch of cynicism. "All you had to do was call 1-800-PRISONS, and they would have told you *exactly* where to reach me."

On the final day of the event, Barnes discussed his ongoing financial struggles with Silna. He bluntly told the former Spirits owner that he didn't think Schupak had treated him fairly back in 1980 when the attorney offered him a $25,000 settlement on the $166,000 he would have been owed in deferred compensation. "I'm leveling with you, Pops. I was all messed up on heroin when I made that deal with Donald. I was so out of my mind that I even brought my dope dealer along to the meeting."

At that point, Silna interrupted. "I know everything that happened. Don't worry, I'll resolve the matter. I'm going to give you all my phone numbers. Call me when you get home, and we'll reach an understanding. Tell me, what do you think it should take to square things? Give me a ballpark figure."

Barnes asked for $30,000.

"OK, then it'll get done," Silna told him. "You've got my word on it. Next time we talk, we'll work out the details."

When Barnes returned to Texas, he encountered a major snag: Silna would not answer or return any of his repeated phone calls for two straight weeks. When they finally did speak, the conversation did not start off well. "Sorry, Marvin, but my lawyers don't want me talking to you. They tell me you're going to be looking to sue me over the circumstances surrounding the settlement you received."

"Pops, I don't work that way. I deal man to man, not lawyer to lawyer. I want to make an agreement with you, period. Then it's over and done with."

"I believe you, and I'm going to trust you. I'll wire you the $30,000 tomorrow."

The money transfer arrived as promised.

Twenty

REACHING OUT TO HELP

The hectic workday was coming to an end at the Golden Eagle Leadership Academy. During his nine-hour shift, Barnes had attended a staff meeting, supervised the morning exercise period, broken up a fistfight, and conducted one-on-one counseling sessions. As he prepared to head home, he was summoned to Quanell X's office, where John Lucas was waiting for him.

"Marvin, I've got a job that only you can handle. Julius Erving needs your help," Lucas said. "His son, Cory, is struggling. He's dropped out of high school and turned to drugs. Doc's sending him here. The young man needs discipline and counseling. More than that, he needs someone to be in his corner, someone he can completely trust. You're that guy. Can you handle it?"

Before accepting the responsibility, Barnes asked several questions. "And this is what Doc wants? He knows I'll be reaching out?"

"He's the one who suggested it," Lucas replied. "He thinks that if Cory can relate to anyone, it's you."

That night, Marvin and Donna phoned Julius and his wife, Turquoise, at their home in Florida to assure them they would do everything in their power to provide guidance and emotional support for their son. "I'm so glad Cory will be there with you," Turquoise said, "and I'm at peace now because I'm sure my baby will be safe, that you'll give him the love he needs."

Despite the Ervings' optimistic outlook, their son was facing one of the most difficult challenges of his life at Golden Eagle, which was not a place for the meek. The toughest, strongest, and most violent adolescents—carjackers, thieves, gang members, and drug pushers—were at the top of the food chain and grew up in the most crime-infested area of the city, the Fifth Ward. In fact, the youths from that district who resided at the academy referred to themselves as members of the "Fifth Ward Hit Squad."

There obviously would be no mercy for Cory, a child of privilege. If the seventeen-year-old showed any signs of weakness, he would be the target of every ruffian at the reform school. "I knew this young man wasn't a wise guy, a punk, or a thug," Barnes said. "From what Julius had told me, his son was quiet and respectful. I was almost positive those qualities were going to work against him at Golden Eagle."

The day before Cory was due to arrive, Marvin rounded up all the alpha dogs at the academy, took them aside, and told them, "The kid who'll be coming in is my friend's son. Treat him right, and I'll help you out. I'll buy you cigarettes, get you day passes, and cover for you if you screw up. You got my word. Cross me, and you'll regret it every time you see my face. Just keep in mind that I can fuck with you forever if you give me a reason."

The overt warning had no effect whatsoever. Solely because Cory was the son of the famous Doctor J and the spitting image of his father, with his neatly cropped Afro, huge hands, good looks, and pleasant smile, he was constantly harassed. More disturbing, Quanell X did nothing to prevent the intimidation. On the contrary, the radical twenty-seven-year-old program director encouraged it because he considered Julius to be an Uncle

Tom, an athlete who became wealthy by kowtowing to the white team owners and executives, the white coaches, and, last but not least, the white fans. "X flat out told me that black ballplayers in the NBA were tap dancing for white folks just to rake in big paychecks," Barnes said. "According to him, we were all nothing more than Stepin Fetchits."

Quanell X's remarks were enough for Barnes to contemplate quitting his job at the academy as soon as Cory completed the program. "All the staff members who worked there resented the kid because they were jealous of Doc's success, both as an athlete and a businessman," Barnes said. "To their way of thinking, Doc wasn't really part of black society because he had crossed the line by disregarding racial boundaries."

The daily abuse endured by the teenager became so devastating that Barnes, with the permission of the Ervings, removed him from Golden Eagle after two weeks and brought him home to live temporarily with Donna, Mel, and himself.

"If I didn't get him away from that place, Cory was going to get jumped and beaten to a pulp. Things were already out of control. No mistaking what was coming next."

Out of harm's way, the introverted youth slowly began to unburden himself, freely discussing his inability to be accepted by his peers and also mentioning how he couldn't even feel at ease in his own home. "I could see he was in pain and I wanted to help. I just wasn't sure how to do it."

One evening, the over-the-hill forty-five-year-old brought Cory to a local high school gym to shoot a few baskets. "I remember watching him practice for the first time and thinking, 'This kid's got some skills. With some decent coaching, he could blossom.' He was like a young racehorse just getting his legs," Barnes would later say. "He had 'hops,' not like his father, of course, but he had a smooth gait, with the same long strides as Julius."

For the next two weeks, Barnes spent an hour each day rebounding for the 6-foot-2 aspiring athlete whose shooting ability and confidence were steadily growing.

Pleased with the progress he had seen, Barnes called Lucas and asked him to evaluate Cory's game. "Why don't you stop by the gym and take a look at the kid?" he said. "He's got potential. He just needs someone who knows how to bring him along."

When the former NBA coach showed up, he watched the youngster work out for no more than 10 minutes. Then he leaned over to Barnes and whispered, 'You've got to be joking. That boy can't play."

"I was so pissed off at Lucas and his know-it-all attitude that I got up and walked away from him," Barnes said later. "Right away, Cory sensed what was going on. I could see that his spirit had been broken."

"That's how it always goes," the disheartened youth told Marvin on the ride home. "No one except my family gives me any props. It's frustrating, you know?"

No matter what sport Cory happened to be playing, the other kids openly rooted against him simply because of his last name, which, in Barnes's opinion, is why the youth originally turned to drugs. Sadly, the sensitive teenager believed a line of coke or a joint would at least provide an hour or so of solace.

"The truth is all Cory wanted was to be like any other kid, no more, no less," Barnes said. "Don't get me wrong: He was proud to be Doc's son, but at the same time, he wanted to be his own man. Just never happened, no matter how hard he tried."

Although Cory was receiving loving support from Marvin and Donna, he still required additional professional counseling. Barnes phoned Julius and Turquoise and told them about a treatment program in Houston—one he himself had completed—that could provide the necessary therapy. With the Ervings' blessing,

Marvin accompanied the youngster to the facility and helped him adjust to his new surroundings.

Placing Cory in that particular rehab did not turn out well because, within days, he relapsed, having smoked marijuana that had been secretly supplied to him by his own counselor. When both their drug tests came back positive, the employee was fired. Cory disappeared hours later, and the police were summoned to search for him. After being apprised of the situation, Barnes drove around the city, hoping to find him unharmed. Donna, meanwhile, remained at home, waiting anxiously by the phone in case Cory called. It took half a day, but authorities finally discovered the runaway youth hiding under a pile of dirty clothes in a closet at his ex-counselor's apartment.

Concerned about their son's state of mind, the Ervings decided to bring him home. Before leaving Houston, Cory called Marvin. During the conversation, they discussed the importance of trust and friendship. "I let him know he didn't have to go it alone," Barnes said. "I told him to call me whenever he wanted to talk, but I never heard from him again."

Fifteen months after returning to Florida, Cory, who had been working at a Panera Bread store while taking courses at Seminole County Community College to earn his high school equivalency diploma, went missing. He had last been seen on May 28, 2000, after leaving Panera, where he had bought sandwiches for a Memorial Day family picnic.

Despite the Ervings' tearful appeals to the public for help and their offer of a $50,000 reward for information leading to Cory's safe return, investigators were unable to uncover any leads in the case for 39 days.

On July 6, while divers from the Seminole County Sheriff's Department were searching the murky waters of an eight-foot deep retention pond next to a dirt road only a half-mile from the Erving home in Sanford, Cory's remains were found inside his submerged 1999 black Volkswagen Passat. Detectives concluded he had taken a shortcut home and lost control of his car, which plunged to the bottom of the pond. Tragically, he had been unable to escape from the vehicle. The drowning death was ruled an accident.

Upon learning of the sad news, Barnes phoned Silna, who knew Julius well, to inform him of what had happened. "I want you and Donna to represent me at the services. I'll take care of all your travel and hotel arrangements," the ex-Spirits owner said. "Please express my condolences to Julius, Turquoise, and the entire family."

At the funeral service held at the Heartland Memorial Church in Kissimmee, Florida, more than 1,500 mourners paid their respects. There were many past and present pro players, coaches, and team executives, as well as classmates of Cory and friends of the family in attendance. The public was also invited as a way of acknowledging all the love and support that the Ervings had been shown throughout the ordeal.

Grammy Award–winning recording artist Patti LaBelle, a close friend of the family, began her tribute to Cory by telling the congregation that he was her "little sweetheart." Then she sang "The Lord's Prayer" a cappella, her powerful voice quivering at times. Orlando Magic executive Pat Williams and Steadman Graham, Oprah Winfrey's boyfriend, both gave heartrending speeches. Cory's siblings, despite dealing with their personal grief, expressed their love for him.

After the rites had concluded, the devastated family stood in front of the congregation and thanked everyone for their many acts of kindness and sympathy. As Julius struggled to say a few words, emotions overwhelmed him. Sitting in the back of the church, Marvin immediately reached for Donna's hand. Together they walked up the center aisle. "When we reached Doc, I extended my arms and gave him a hug," Barnes recalled. "He put his head on my shoulder and began to cry. Turq, who'd been embracing Donna, grabbed our hands and whispered, 'Thank you both. Cory loved you two so very much.'"

Although an autopsy revealed trace amounts of cocaine in Cory's system, Barnes knew in his heart that the teenager would have eventually succeeded in defeating his demons. "I'm sure of it because I know the type of person he was. It's possible he might have gone on to lose a few more battles, but he never would've stopped fighting. Cory wasn't a quitter."

Twenty-One

A STRAIGHT TALK WITH GOD

Major health issues began to surface in 2000 as Barnes approached two and a half years of sobriety. A doctor in Houston diagnosed him as suffering from severe liver disease, most likely caused by decades of recurrent drug abuse. "Listening to all the medical mumbo jumbo," he said, "I thought I was a goner."

Still, the forty-eight-year-old, who was now working at the Prospect House Fulfillment Center, a sober living facility, attempted to maintain an optimistic attitude. "I'd always been told that God doesn't give you anything you can't handle. At least that's what I tried to convince myself. I talked to a million shrinks and attended all my AA and NA meetings, but what I really needed was guidance from above. Unfortunately, I thought that God and I had gone our separate ways a long time ago. Since I already had one foot in the grave, I figured that I might as well go out with a bang."

After forging and cashing one of his wife's personal checks, Barnes disappeared into the bowels of Houston. Worried about his deteriorating health, as well as his safety, Donna drove around the city every night for two weeks attempting to track him down. Finally, a young woman told her that she remembered seeing a "very tall, very drunk" black man near Old Spanish Trail and Scott Street. Arriving at the location, Donna spotted Marvin, shirtless and mumbling gibberish, as he paced back and forth in front of a Walgreens. Pleading and crying, she somehow talked him into returning home.

"I don't think he had eaten so much as a ham sandwich in all the time he'd been missing," Donna says. "He had traded his good shoes for a pair of old ones, which were at least three full sizes too small for him, and some crack."

Her successful rescue efforts failed to curtail Marvin's drug habit. To obtain enough money for his daily coke supply, he began stealing Donna's possessions. While she was at work, he pawned her jewelry and swiped all her dresses, selling them on the streets to prostitutes.

"I was driving home from work one afternoon," she says, "and I saw a young woman in high heels standing on a street corner. She was wearing an outfit that looked exactly like one I owned. When I got home, I looked in the bedroom closet. Everything of mine was gone. I just broke down, not because Marvin had stolen and sold my property, but because I realized how desperate he had become to get his hands on drug money."

The thievery went far beyond personal items. Barnes even pawned the couple's microwave oven and camera. To prevent him from selling their new 34-inch color TV, Donna lugged it to her car and lifted it into the trunk every morning before leaving for work. When she returned from her job each evening, she would struggle to carry the set back into the apartment.

After watching powerlessly as her husband turned into a mindless zombie, Donna, as a last resort, had him committed. Two muscle-bound cops were dispatched to the apartment where Marvin, who had been hallucinating after smoking black tar heroin, was wrestled to the floor, subdued, and placed in a straitjacket. Transported to Ben Taub General Hospital, he was escorted to a padded room on the mental health ward. When a nurse weighed him, he was an anemic 149 pounds.

Following a five-day evaluation period, Barnes was informed that he had the legal right to check himself out, which he opted to do. In a moment of clarity, he placed a call to Silna. Remembering the commitment the former Spirits owner had made to offer help no matter what the circumstances, Marvin confessed that he was using and also revealed that medical tests had shown he was dying from liver disease.

"Doctors can be wrong, you know," Silna said. "You need to get a second opinion from a specialist. I'll get you the best. Just stay off the cocaine and whatever else you're putting into your system."

That same day, Silna arranged for Barnes to be examined by the foremost internal medicine expert in Houston. When test results came back a week after the appointment, there was an encouraging prognosis. The illness was not terminal, providing Barnes would faithfully take four prescription medicines daily and immediately stop using all opiates. He was also informed that Silna would be picking up the tab for all the doctors' bills, as well as for the necessary drugs, which would cost approximately $600 a month.

It was the best news possible, a life-saving opportunity, yet Barnes could not break away from the spell of cocaine. Sensing that her son was ignoring the specialist's order to cease all drug use, Lula sent his sister to check up on him.

On the morning of her flight, Alfreda called to say she would be arriving at Marvin's apartment around 5 p.m., but when she showed up at the prearranged time, he was nowhere to be found. For four hours she waited fretfully with Donna. At last, he lurched through the door, completely loaded on crack. Seeing her brother so strung out and emaciated, Alfreda burst into tears and held him close to her. Marvin's childhood protector was once more at his side, determined to watch over him.

For the next two days, she visited rehab centers in the metropolitan Houston area, trying without success to get her brother into a program. Unfortunately, he was persona non grata at each one, having thrown away repeated chances to regain his sobriety. As Lucas said when Barnes first sought his assistance, "You can't *make* addicts get straight. If they're not one hundred percent committed to seeking help, they're lost causes."

Meanwhile, Donna had learned from a family member about a so-called miracle treatment for addicts in Portsmouth, Virginia, where her parents lived. Marvin, recognizing that his next "slip" could be his last, arranged to have his probation transferred and agreed to enter the innovative program, which was named "Victory in Jesus."

At the first meeting with his new parole officer, Barnes volunteered a confession. "Don't even bother drug testing me because the results are going to come back dirty. But I'm getting help. I've found a treatment program that really works. It's called Victory in Jesus. You got my word that I'm going to stay clean for good this time."

The court officer took mercy on him and skipped the mandated screening.

Frail, and foggy, Barnes eased himself into the counseling sessions held at the Mount Carmel Missionary Baptist Church, attending a meeting or two each week. After a month, he became a nightly visitor. "I've gone through every kind of therapy imaginable," he told award-winning *Virginian-Pilot* columnist Ed Miller. "Turns out what I never tried was having a straight talk with God. I always told myself I wasn't ready for religion because I had some wild times still ahead of me. I figured a relationship with God would only get in the way of my fun.

"Most rehab treatments fail because they don't fill the void that is left when you give up drugs or alcohol. Victory in Jesus fills me up with God's love. Now I know there isn't anyone, no matter what they've done, who can't be saved."

His renewed faith in redemption was kindled by the Reverend E. T. Knight, founder of the counseling program. "I saw people come into the church who had no self-esteem," Barnes said. "The pastor turned them all into God's soldiers. When I started thinking about all the people I hurt, all the money I blew, and all the damage I did to my body, I understood that only a higher power could have gotten me through those experiences. The reverend showed me that God must have a plan for me because there has to be a reason why I'm still here on this earth."

When discussing substance abuse with fellow members of Victory in Jesus, Barnes cited his own countless failures as examples of how the devil is always lying in wait. His words were succinct. "The bible tells us that Satan deceives, steals, and destroys," he told Pastor Knight's followers. "Well, cocaine does the devil's work. It deceives by convincing you that it makes you feel stronger, it steals by taking away your self-respect, and it destroys by tearing down your body and mind. If you don't fight to get clean, you'll be left with nothing."

Before long, Barnes took his message to the streets, serving as the pastor's "apostle." He had a sixth sense when it came to spotting someone struggling to overcome a personal problem. With an innate ability to strike up a heart-to-heart conversation with total strangers, he offered comfort and hope by recounting the lowlights of his own decades of despair and loneliness.

His caring and humble approach produced remarkable results. Every week, he would bring new guests to Victory in Jesus. Most of them became regulars at the group's meetings. "Marvin had a gift for showing folks that they were loved. He greeted everybody the same way: with a smile, a hug, and a few encouraging words," says Reverend Knight. "He was doing God's work and making a difference in people's lives."

The reborn Christian might have remained in Virginia had it not been for a telephone call he received one evening from his mother, informing him that his father was dying. After hearing the news, he caught the next plane to Providence. It was time to bid a final farewell to Al, whom he had not seen since 1975.

Arriving in time to join his mother and sister as they stood and prayed next to Al's hospital bed, Marvin tenderly kissed Lula. Then he opened his father's eyes with his thumbs and told the man he had despised for so long that he had forgiven him. Seconds later, Al flatlined.

Because the family did not have enough money to pay for the funeral and burial expenses, Barnes phoned Silna to ask for help.

"I'll take care of everything," Silna said. "Tell me, did you make peace with your father before he died?"

"Yes, I did," Barnes replied. "I got to say goodbye to him in my own way."

"Good, that was important for both of you. Now, when you go to the funeral home, have the owner call me, and I'll make the financial arrangements."

After the payment details had been worked out, Barnes called his benefactor to thank him again. "Marvin, my memory isn't what it used to be. Is this the fourth or the fifth time that your father has died and you've gotten me to send you money for the funeral?" Silna said, using a touch of humor to ease the burden of losing a parent.

Rather than returning to the Victory in Jesus program, Barnes remained in Providence, principally because he was able to find work as a youth counselor. The opportunity came about after the Providence basketball staff had invited him to speak at the school's summer camp. His appearance was covered by both local TV stations and the *Providence Journal*, which lauded his no-holds-barred style of delivering a poignant message about drugs and crime. Donna, meanwhile, decided to part ways with Marvin on good terms, staying behind in Virginia to care for her ailing mother.

Before long, Barnes was being invited to talk to teenagers throughout the state. He knew he was delivering a powerful, important statement, but he wanted to do more than merely give speeches. With the financial backing of the Silna brothers, he established the Rebound Foundation in the fall of 2001. The purpose of the charitable organization was to provide counseling to at-risk juveniles in the Greater Providence area. The Silnas donated a new Lincoln Navigator to the foundation, paid rent for an office, purchased two computers, bought a condominium where Barnes could live rent-free, and provided him with a weekly salary of $700.

Former Providence teammates and coaches, as well as politicians, attorneys, and prominent businessmen, were recruited to serve on the foundation's board of directors. In less than three months, Rebound opened its doors. One of the non-profit charity's first projects was the creation of a program called "Men to Men," in which high school students were mentored by successful community leaders at the Metropolitan Regional Career and Technical Center on Public Street. City officials, police officers, pro athletes, judges, and corporate CEOs all enthusiastically accepted invitations to be guest speakers.

Barnes's work with the foundation went above and beyond running the after-school program.

Using his own personal funds, he'd regularly treat his students to a meal at a nearby restaurant. "Most of my kids had it rough at home. Their dinners were usually macaroni and cheese, franks and beans, pizza, or, if they were lucky, Kentucky Fried Chicken. For them, going out to a nice place and ordering whatever they wanted was a huge deal."

In addition, Barnes proved to be a persuasive solicitor, making cold calls at clothing stores throughout the city and convincing proprietors to donate jackets, shoes, boots, gloves, and hats to underprivileged children.

He also made it his mission to procure after-school employment for teenagers who came from financially struggling families by establishing a job bank, working with city agencies, and handing out flyers to as many private business owners as possible.

As the Men to Men executive director tooled around town in his black SUV that had a spare tire cover which read "Rebound: The Spirit of Giving," it was not uncommon for a total stranger to call out, "Hey, Maah-vin, real proud of you."

As word of the foundation's good work continued to spread, checks from corporations, as well as individuals, began to roll in. These were extraordinary times for Barnes, who had not only regained his dignity but become an inspiration to the entire community.

But, as with everything in his life, Bad News soon lost sight of his goal.

Four years after the doors opened, the good name of Rebound would be smeared by the actions of its founder when Barnes cut back on his work schedule and went on a quest for cocaine. "I honestly can't explain why I did it. Maybe I thought I could get away with taking a one-day break from staying sober," he would later say, "or maybe it was because, like Donna had told me back in Houston, I was afraid to succeed."

Now willing to do absolutely anything for quick cash, he phoned Silna and managed to dupe him into sending $3,000 for a Rebound project, which, in reality, was nonexistent.

Alfreda, knowing full well that her brother was once again using, somehow managed to obtain Ozzie's private phone number and called him. "Please don't send any more money to my brother," she begged. "I know you mean well, but the cash you're giving him isn't being used for the foundation. It's all going up his nose. That's what's going on here, no matter what bullshit he's telling you. What you're doing is enabling him."

The astute businessman with the generous heart was shattered by such a calculated act of betrayal.

Unaware of his sister's intervention, Marvin, running out of cash to fuel his habit, called Ozzie a few days later.

"I don't have much time. What's on your mind?" Silna asked, sounding unusually stiff and abrupt.

"Well, Pops, I could use a few hundred bucks. The SUV needs some repairs and I'm a little low on cash."

Silna had heard enough. "Marvin, stop. I know you're conning me. I know you're on drugs again, and that means you're letting down a lot of kids who believe in you. Stop bothering me. And don't call me Pops. I hardly know your mother, and

I certainly have never slept with her. Find someone else to pester. I'm through with you."

All the lies and scams had finally caught up with Bad News.

On December 22, 2005, Barnes was arrested at his Warwick, Rhode Island, condominium for domestic disorderly conduct. Two cops found him naked on his balcony, screaming obscenities at his girlfriend. According to police, there wasn't any physical violence and no drugs were found. However, one officer noted in his official report that "the male resident admitted to using cocaine a few days ago." The misdemeanor charges were dropped three weeks later. Shortly thereafter, Barnes was evicted from his residence.

Not surprisingly, he was arrested again on May 15, 2006, for felony cocaine possession. A Rhode Island judge ordered him to either serve a year in prison or enter a 90-day rehab program. He chose the latter, with his lone expectation being that undergoing therapy would be a colossal waste of time.

Not a single relative or friend believed a stay at Treatment Solutions of South Florida in Pompano Beach, Florida, would have any long-term benefit for Barnes. This was, after all, the twentieth time he had entered rehab, which, Marvin joked, was probably a record of some sort. "Getting sober when you're stuck in a facility is easy," he once said. "Staying sober afterward is when I always had major problems."

Counselors showed the habitual drug abuser no empathy and offered him little hope. "There's nothing I can tell you that you haven't heard before," one of them told Barnes. "You'll say all the right things and try to get over on us every chance you get. You're an old pro at this. You'll sail through. But trust me, once you leave this place, you won't be able to hack it in the real world because you're nothing but a fuck-up."

"It was one putdown after another," Barnes said. "They kept telling me I was beyond help. I'd say something about being determined to get clean, and they'd sit there and laugh in my face. If this was their idea of rehabilitation, I wanted out. I seriously thought of bolting, but where the hell would I go? If I went on the run and got caught, I'd have to spend another year of my life behind bars. There really was no choice but to hang in there while everyone took turns mocking me."

In the opinion of counselors, Marvin, an addict for thirty years, wasn't going to change. His modus operandi had always been the same: get clean, get out, get wasted. The whole futile process was his twisted version of *Groundhog Day*, with the same pathetic plot being replayed time and time again.

Returning to Providence after completing rehab, Barnes underwent mandatory drug testing for six months, with the results always coming back negative. Once the testing period expired, however, he resumed his love affair with crack cocaine, just as the team of rehab therapists had predicted.

"Over the years, it's been so sad and frustrating to see the guy destroy himself," said Barnes's basketball brother, Ernie D. "When you talk about his problems, what you have to keep in mind is that the only person he really ever hurts is himself. His friends get on his case all the time, but not one of us ever gives up on him because we know all the good he has deep down inside.

"Marvin tries to convince himself that he can do drugs and still live forever. I remember him telling me that a doctor once told him that every time a person snorts cocaine, 100,000 brain cells are destroyed. Then he smiled at me and said, 'With all the thousands of times I used coke over the years and all the millions of brain cells that I killed off, I must have been born a damn genius.'"

Despite being able to make light of his addiction, Barnes realized he needed to make drastic changes in his life. "I'd been hanging around Providence, getting into a few jams," he said later. "A car dealer gave me a loaner, and I let a girl use it for a few days in return for some coke. When she and the car disappeared, the auto dealer called the cops. They were all set to bag me for grand larceny until Alfreda managed to find the girl and brought the car back. After that, I knew that if didn't try to get straight somehow, someway, I was going to go off the deep end and do something else crazy that would land me back in prison."

He decided to relocate to Framingham, Massachusetts, where he rented a studio apartment. Less than a week after he had moved in, Barnes, contrite and silent, walked into an Alcoholic Anonymous meeting at the local Salvation Army.

Accompanied by his future sponsor, a man called Big Ike, he arrived 25 minutes late for the 7 a.m. gathering. None of the regular attendees seemed to notice as the paunchy, bald giant eased himself into a rickety wooden folding chair in the back row of seats.

As soon as the meeting ended, the approximately thirty participants broke off into small informal groups to discuss their personal successes, failures, and everyday lives. Most were dressed in business attire, but some wore second-hand clothes, which were either too large or too small. Despite their diverse backgrounds, they all shared the daily battle of attempting to conquer their addictions. Barnes, looking much older than his fifty-five years, remained slumped in his chair, lost in thought as he bowed his head while taking stock of his life. After a few minutes, he struggled to stand on gimpy knees, adjusted his frayed Red Sox cap, and limped toward a coffee machine.

The newcomer to the group took but a few steps before someone with a high-pitched voice began to make a commotion.

"I knew it," shouted a middle-aged Hispanic man, pointing and waving his arms frenetically. "It's him. It's Marvin Barnes, the baddest basketball player ever to come out of New England. Providence College. All-American. Pro superstar. The greatest scorer and rebounder I've ever seen, bar none."

The room paused to gawk as the white-whiskered stranger filled his Dunkin' Donuts coffee cup. Clearly embarrassed, he made brief eye contact, waved off the unwanted attention with a flick of his right hand, and quickly slipped out a back door.

Walking down a deserted side street with Big Ike, Barnes joked about the rousing welcome he had just received. "Well, so much for the Anonymous part of AA," the bankrupt ex-ballplayer said. "I knew I'd be recognized, but I didn't expect some wild man to be trippin' like that. I was waiting for him to get a camera so he could have his picture taken with me. You can be sure that'll happen when I show up tomorrow. Bet he'll want a few autographs, too. But, hey, at least I'm still remembered."

For the next six years, Barnes kept his vow not to use drugs or alcohol. No longer did he place much value in the ancient basketball trophies, dusty award plaques, and faded yellow newspaper clippings that had been stored in cardboard boxes. Instead, his most prized possessions, the half-dozen metal-plated chips he had received at AA to commemorate the anniversaries of his sobriety, were always kept in his right front pants pocket as a constant reminder of his achievements.

At the group assemblies, Barnes was both observant and compassionate, commanding the room like a seasoned politician. He had a knack for remembering names and took the time to make sure his fellow 12-steppers were all staying on the righteous path. "When I see someone who is in pain, I give them my phone number and tell them to call me day or night if they want to talk privately. I need these meetings. I need to go to church. They're both sanctuaries for sinners, and I've definitely committed more than my fair share of sins."

Twenty-Two

"THE RACE"

When Providence College officials announced that Barnes's basketball jersey would be raised to the rafters at the Dunkin' Donuts Center on March 8, 2008, the alumni reaction was predictably mixed. Some believed the honor was decades overdue; others thought such a tribute should never take place, not for a three-time convicted felon.

Despite a flurry of negative publicity, the school stood firm. As the ceremony date approached, the 1974 All-American was asked to select someone who had a meaningful impact on his life to introduce him at the alumni's awards banquet, which was to be held on the night before the jersey ceremony. Without hesitation, Barnes chose Allan Baker, his college teammate and roommate, to deliver the speech because they shared far more than fond memories of their four years as Friars: the close friends were both recovering cocaine addicts.

At age fifty-two, Baker, a senior vice president at multibillion-dollar financial conglomerate ING and a member of Providence College's Board of Trustees, was forced to resign from both positions after he had become hooked on coke and was caught red-handed making a buy in a Hartford, Connecticut, suburb in 2004.

By day, the 6-foot-6 former power forward for the Friars had been a wealthy corporate executive, highly respected as a church-going family man and a role model in the African American community. By night, he had been known simply as "Big Al with the Mercedes" or "Uncle Al," code names given to him by his street dealers. Foolishly, he had thought he was too intelligent, too mentally strong to allow the white powder to become the focus of his life.

The media scrutiny intensified when in late 2005, a federal grand jury handed down an indictment against the humiliated recipient of three honorary doctorate degrees, charging him with conspiracy to buy and distribute more than five grams of the drug. On TV stations throughout New England, Baker's secret life was the top story on the 11 p.m. news. The banner headline in the *Providence Journal* read "Ex-PC Cager Faces Trial on Drug Charges," while the *Hartford Courant*'s front-page article was entitled "Another Side of a Go-To Guy."

Through rehab, prayer, and the unwavering support of family and friends, Baker eventually regained his sobriety and self-respect.

Although the fallen former business leader had been drug-free for more than three years, many Providence administrators were openly critical of the athletic department's decision to allow him to speak at the school-sponsored event. In fact, Barnes's former coach, Dave Gavitt, did his best to sway the Friars' all-time leading rebounder into making a more politically correct choice. "You're asking for trouble, Marvin," he said. "The alumni are going to say, 'That's just great. PC's got one addict introducing another.'"

Barnes, however, refused to budge.

So when Baker, head held high, strode across the stage to deliver his address at the podium, the atmosphere in the packed

Westin Hotel ballroom was eerily tense. No one in the audience was quite sure what to expect. Most assumed he would play it safe, running down the list of Barnes's basketball accomplishments and reminiscing about PC's 1973 Final Four season. Instead, the highly experienced public speaker surprised everyone by discussing "The Race," a poem by D. H. Groberg that dealt with overcoming adversity. The concluding verses read as follows:

So anxious to restore himself, to catch up and to win,
His mind went faster than his legs; he slipped and fell again.
He wished that he had quit before with only one disgrace,
"I'm hopeless as a runner now, I shouldn't try to race."
But through the laughing crowd he searched and found his father's face.
With a steady look that said again, "Get up and win that race!"

So he jumped up to try again, ten yards behind the last.
"If I'm to gain those yards," he thought, "I've got to run real fast."
Exceeding everything he had, he regained eight, then ten . . .
But trying hard to catch the lead, he slipped and fell again.
"I've lost so what's the use?" he thought. "I'll live with my disgrace."
But then he thought about his dad, who soon he'd have to face.
"Get up," an echo sounded low, "you haven't lost at all,
For all you have to do to win is rise each time you fall."
Three times he'd fallen stumbling, three times he rose again.
Too far behind to hope to win, he still ran to the end.
They cheered another boy who crossed the line and won first place,
Head high and proud and happy—no falling, no disgrace.

But when the fallen youngster crossed the line, in last place,
The crowd gave him a greater cheer for finishing the race.

And to his dad he sadly said, "I didn't do so well."
"To me, you won," his father said. "You rose each time you
fell."

As soon as the moving speech had ended, Barnes leaned over to
DiGregorio, who was also being honored that night, and said,
"Damn, that's me. I'm that little kid. And I'm still running the
race, baby."

Encouraged by the warm, unbridled show of support he had
received at the event, Barnes ramped up his efforts to rebuild the
Rebound Foundation and its Men to Men program. Although
almost all of the charity's former backers were no longer willing
to dig deep for donations, Ozzie Silna was still on board, agreeing
to provide the necessary funding to get the organization up and
running again.

"I have a calling in life," Barnes said. "I'm never going to be
rich, but Rebound's message is going to come across loud and
clear. Providence is a rough town. You got gangs, you got crime,
and you got unemployment and poverty. With today's economy
being so shaky, the West End reminds me of when I was growing
up. Walk through my old neighborhood and you still see board-
ed-up stores on almost every other block and houses that no one
in their right mind would want to live in. The kids in my program
will face the same problems I did back in the sixties. They need a
reason to have hope. They need to understand that they can make
something of themselves if they get an education and stay out of
trouble."

After restarting the Men to Men program, Barnes not only
brought in civic leaders and pro athletes as speakers, but sought

out people he referred to as the devil's helpers—thieves, drug addicts and pushers, former gang bangers, and ex-cons—to give scared straight talks to the teenagers.

One guest lecturer, a thirty-five-year-old former heroin user, told of having contracted Hepatitis C from contaminated needles. "It can take years for the symptoms to show," he said. "By then, your liver's shot and your skin is turning yellow. Once you get the virus, you'll always be a carrier."

A baby-faced former petty thief, only twenty-four years old, painfully recalled the fear he experienced while incarcerated at ACI. Voice trembling, he compared his relatively short stay in prison to witnessing a series of pit bull attacks. "These guys go for the throat and they don't let go. I saw violence every single day. You're scared shitless, but you can't show it. You have to watch your back 24/7 because you can't trust anybody. Is that really what you want for yourself?"

Barnes fully realized the stories of brutality were traumatic for the teenagers to hear. "But I want to keep things raw," he said. "My kids have to understand the consequences of hanging with the wrong crowd. They need to see that prisons are deathtraps. I want them to know there's no such thing as a 'friend' behind bars. When you're locked up, your life could be snuffed out because of a small disagreement or just because someone might not like how you handle yourself."

To demonstrate the animalistic viciousness that can occur on a cellblock, Barnes showed his students a grainy video of a black inmate being stabbed sixty-seven times by a white prisoner. "It was gruesome. Some of my kids couldn't watch the whole thing. But I wanted to drive home my point, so I played it for them again. Every one of them wanted to leave, but I wouldn't let them until they watched the entire attack. When it was over, I raised my voice and told the kids, "Life ain't no damn dress rehearsal.

You get one chance to do things right. You screw up and, in seconds, your life can be taken away.'"

Another time the class was introduced to a parolee who had served six years for assault. The thirty-seven-year-old felon told his story in a few sentences. "I ran with a tough crowd and thought I had to show people I was a bad ass. By the time I was eighteen, my future was ruined. You can't get involved with crime, even minor things, because once you start making stupid decisions, you won't stop until you land in prison for something big, just like I did."

When one of the students timidly asked whether homosexual activity really occurred in prison, the ex-con, with the impassive, wide-eyed look of a madman, said, "When it comes to life in a cellblock, a lot of inmates doing years and years of hard time figure they've got to make do with what's available. Does that answer your question?"

Barnes also brought his pupils to a funeral home where the owner described the unforgettable aura of pain and sadness at wakes held for teenagers who had died as a result of street violence. "I see the shock on the parents' faces. There are no words that can comfort them," the undertaker said. "It's impossible for them to comprehend how their sons and daughters could end up in a coffin at such a young age. The worst thing is that these wakes occur far too frequently—and still the bloodshed continues. None of it makes any sense to me. The most difficult part of my job is when I look down at the body of a victim and realize this child will have no more tomorrows."

David Banda, who today is a residential case manager at the Providence Center, was in Barnes's first Men to Men program. "Getting to meet a sports legend was a thrill, but once we understood what the program was all about, the hero worshiping stopped. Mr. Barnes—that's what we called him out of respect—was no longer a celebrity; he was our mentor. He made it clear he was there for a serious reason: to show us through his own experiences why making poor choices in life will destroy you bit by bit."

Of all the speakers who participated in the program, the one who impressed Banda the most was Barnes himself. "He was ultra-intense," the twenty-two-year-old social worker says. "He called himself an idiot for ever getting involved in crime, drugs, and gangs. Before and after each class, he'd talk privately to students about how they were doing in school and at home. No matter what problems we had, he was willing to help."

Christian Quinonez, who was a straight-A senior at the Met School, also attended Men to Men classes. Now a full-time teaching assistant in the Providence school system, he plans to earn an education degree from the University of Rhode Island. "Mr. Barnes did so much for me and all the students in Men to Men. He told us over and over again that if we have a personal problem, go talk with him or any other counselor at the school. He reminded us over and over again that there's never any shame in asking for help."

Approximately twice a month, Barnes spoke at Rhode Island schools, basketball camps, and juvenile detention centers. At one such event held at Central Falls High, two hundred upper classmen gazed up at the relaxed, smiling lecturer as he stood alone on a stage. For the first five minutes of his address, he was articulate and soft spoken, introducing himself by describing his past life as a wealthy basketball star. Once he had captured the attention of his audience, he abruptly morphed into Bad News, the former juvenile delinquent, the ex-con, the homeless person, the recovering drug addict. Shifting into the language of the ghetto and liberally using street terms to emphasize the inevitably grim consequences of being a "thug," he spared no details as he recounted his mortifying experiences.

"I was a dope," he said as he moved slowly up and down the aisles of the school's auditorium, staring into the eyes of random adolescents. "I thought drugs were cool. But drugs took away my future and left me with nothing. Think using cocaine or marijuana makes you cool? Ain't a damn thing cool about being locked up in a cage.

"You think you're tough? You have no idea what tough is until you spend time in prison. I was behind bars for five years, and each and every day I saw violence."

His voice filled with emotion, Barnes told of having visited the son of a neighborhood friend in a hospital. "The kid—he was about your age—had been shot in the head the night before. When I went to see him, he was in a coma, not expected to make it. I stood next to him and noticed he had the words "THUG LIFE" tattooed on his right arm. Let me tell you, thug life is a game that's designed for you to lose.

"The same young man I just told you about had $1,700 in his wallet when he got shot, probably money he'd got by pushing drugs. What good is all that cash to him now that he's lying in a hospital bed with a bullet lodged in his brain?

"Everybody starts using weed, coke, or booze to have a good time with their boys. But I'm here to tell you that no matter how close a drug abuser is to his friends, there are two things he's going to have to face alone: prison and death."

The Men to Men program was receiving widespread recognition from public officials, the media, and the students themselves. One glowing article in the *Providence Journal* caught the attention of an executive with a New York–based speakers bureau, who after viewing a videotape of one of Barnes's riveting ad-lib talks, sent him a contract proposal. In addition, he was contacted by the NBA Retired Players Association, which was interested in discussing a possible job opportunity.

Perhaps the biggest ego booster came in October of 2013, when ESPN released *Free Spirits*, a 30 for 30 documentary directed by ten-time Emmy Award–winner Dan Forer. The one-hour film chronicled the two-year existence of the ABA's Spirits of St. Louis and prominently featured numerous vignettes about Barnes's immense talent and his oftentimes outrageous conduct.

Given all the encouraging recent developments, the Rebound Foundation president believed the timing was ideal for expansion. "I'm going to bring the Men to Men program to Boston and Worcester," he told a reporter. "I've got community leaders all lined up and ready to come on board."

But the grandiose plans would be shelved due to events that occurred between Wednesday, January 12, and Monday, January 17, 2012.

A potential serious legal matter developed after Barnes, by chance, encountered a female student in a Met High hallway moments before his class was scheduled to begin. During a two-minute conversation, he asked the girl if she was a model. When she replied that it was her goal to pursue a career in that field, the school counselor mentioned that he knew some people who could offer advice.

Before entering his classroom, Barnes handed her a Rebound business card and told her to call him to discuss her ambitions further. Over the next three days, the two exchanged phone calls and text messages.

On Sunday, January 16, the girl—who was seventeen years old—and her mother filed a complaint at the Cranston Police Department headquarters, alleging harassment and inappropriate communication by Barnes. According to a police report, the juvenile said the initial topic of conversation was about modeling but the talk quickly evolved into a discussion "of a sexual nature."

She further alleged that the teacher, as she described Barnes to police, mentioned that if the two of them had sex, he would give her $200. According to the student, he sent her a $50 MoneyGram "to prove he was serious."

On the morning of Monday, January 17, Barnes called the girl's cell phone and asked to meet her at the Coffee Bean Express in Cranston at noon. Before leaving for the appointment, she was wired by police. At the same time, Cranston and Providence detectives were setting up surveillance at the cafe.

After Barnes entered the store, he casually greeted the student and sat down with her at a back table. While they were talking, detectives approached and asked if they could speak to him privately outside.

As soon as Barnes stepped onto the sidewalk, he was taken into custody without incident and transported to the Cranston Police headquarters, where he was read his rights and interrogated.

During his interview with the detectives, Barnes denied making any sexual advances to the girl. Although he acknowledged having wired her $50, he said she had asked him for a $150 personal loan in a text message that he still had saved on his cell phone. "I told her I could help her out with $50 but that she would have to ask her father or someone else for the rest of the money," he stated. According to a police report, the Men to Men program director admitted that the entire situation was "a case of bad judgment" on his part. Despite being confronted with the fact that phone conversations between him and the student had been recorded, Barnes steadfastly denied any wrongdoing. At the conclusion of the questioning, he was charged with one felony count of indecent solicitation of a child and was released on $5,000 personal recognizance.

Following media reports of the arrest, the Met School announced that the Men to Men program was being terminated and that Barnes had been fired. Providence sports talk show callers, except for those who believed in the presumption of innocence, were outraged. "I'm sick and tired of hearing that loser's name," one listener said. "He's an embarrassment. Always has been."

In a telephone interview with an Associated Press reporter, Barnes said the charge against him "were bogus. I didn't meet with the girl to have sex. I don't pursue young girls. I'm not a stalker, a pedophile, or a pervert."

Over the course of the next 18 months, there were numerous postponements of the criminal court case. With each delay, Barnes, who had moved into a spare bedroom at my house in November of 2011, became more agitated. "This whole thing is a setup. She told the cops that she Googled my name on the day she first met me and found out I was a former NBA player. Two days later, she's filing a complaint that I propositioned her. What a crock," he told anyone willing to listen to his version of events. "I need to clear my name and get on with my life."

In early 2014, the pressure of waiting for a trial began to take both a mental and physical toll on Barnes. He broke up with his longtime girlfriend, stopped going to AA and NA meetings, and began to experience major health issues. Twice he was admitted to Framingham Union Hospital for treatment of dangerously high blood pressure and heart palpitations. Following what was supposed to be a routine physical exam by a urologist at the Lahey Clinic in Burlington, Massachusetts, he was ordered to undergo extensive testing, including a biopsy, to determine the cause of consistently elevated PSA levels, a possible indication of prostate cancer.

Full-blown depression began to set in. Hibernating in his room for days at a time, Barnes did little but watch bootleg DVDs and sleep on an unmade bed for up to fourteen hours a day. Piles of dirty clothes, dozens of crushed cigarette packs, and unopened mail, mostly letters from bill collectors, covered his grape juice-stained wall-to-wall carpet. His "meals" consisted of peanut butter and bacon sandwiches or boiled hot dogs, salt and vinegar potato chips, miniature Table Talk pies, orange soda, and an occasional pizza.

For three weeks he kept his cell phone turned off, cutting off all ties to the outside world. The ominous brooding escalated rapidly once Barnes added a six-pack of Heinekens to his daily diet, unsuccessfully attempting to conceal his drinking from me by burying his empties beneath a pile of crumpled newspapers at the bottom of a garbage can.

When I confronted him about his alcohol consumption, he trivialized the matter, one of his standard defensive tactics. "Ain't no big thing. I can handle a couple cans of beer. Don't sweat it."

"You're talking to the wrong guy," I told him. "The first day you moved in here, we made a deal: no drinking, no drugs. My house, my rules. What I'll never understand is why you're willing to throw away six years of sobriety."

His only response was a dismissive shrug of the shoulders.

Several weeks later, Barnes's behavior became even more bizarre. Almost every night he'd leave the house at 10 p.m. and return after sunrise, immediately retreating to his room until the next evening. As I was leaving for work one morning, I observed that his SUV was parked on the street, with its right wheels up on the curb. The motor was running, the satellite radio was blaring, and the driver's door was wide open. Slouched in the reclining seat behind the steering wheel was Barnes, passed out. It took me a full five minutes to wake him, and when he did come to, he was confused and incoherent. When I asked what drug he had been using, he ignored the question and stutter-stepped his way across the lawn and into the house.

That same day I called Damian Farley, a retired DEA agent who had been one of my law enforcement sources, to seek his advice about how to help Barnes. "Look, we're dealing with an epidemic, one that's spreading like wildfire. The estimate is that 50,000 people nationwide will die next year from drug overdoses. In my opinion, that's a conservative projection," he said. "At least once a month I hear from someone I know personally who has a family member hooked on cocaine, meth, heroin, or prescription drugs. Every one of them is in a complete state of panic. They want to know how to get through to their son, their daughter, their spouse, or even a parent. I give them all the same advice: offer support and encouragement, but don't give them any money and don't show the slightest bit of sympathy. Unfortunately, there's nothing anyone can do for an addict until that person hits rock bottom—and there's no way of predicting when that moment may come."

One telltale sign that Barnes was getting high on a daily basis was that he was rapidly accumulating sizeable debts. Despite receiving $1,878 in monthly disability payments from the government, he owed more than $3,000 on his leased SUV and $1,800 on his cell phone, both of which were registered in the name of Rebound.

Of course, he could still rely on Silna for financial assistance. In 2013, the seventy-nine-year-old philanthropist had donated more than $20,000 to the foundation, which, unbeknownst to him, had been inactive for the entire year. And now in spring 2014, Barnes was using the charity's cash reserves as his own personal slush fund, draining every cent from the non-profit's checking account in order to fund his cocaine purchases.

Additionally, he sold his 36-inch Sony HDTV and a two-year-old Hewlett Packard desktop computer for a total of $350. Out of desperation, he pawned his most valued personal possession: a glass-encased red, white, and blue game ball that had been autographed for him by 27 of the 30 all-time greatest players in ABA history at the 1997 reunion in Indianapolis. The unique collector's item fetched only $125.

One night I came home to find Barnes and a grungy stranger smoking crack in my living room. "Marvin, get your dope-dealing pal out of here before I call the cops," I yelled. "I'm tired of you spitting in my face. Either check into rehab or pack your bags."

He apologized the next day and began out-patient treatment at AdCare Hospital in Worcester, Massachusetts. After his second day in the program, he came home with a fellow rehab patient and proceeded to get high. Watching him bounce off the hallway walls, I laced into him.

"You've finally worn me out," I told him. "Obviously, you're not serious about wanting help. Shit, you couldn't even stay straight for forty-eight freaking hours."

"All I did was take a Percocet and a couple Klonopins to help me relax," he said, trying to minimize and mitigate his actions.

"What a crock. Now you're trying to tell me that popping a few pills is harmless. You think I haven't figured out that you're buying prescription meds from somebody? You think I'm believing all your bullshit? Marvin, it's time for you to go."

And with that, Barnes packed a suitcase and left without saying a word.

Two weeks later, he called me from AdCare, where he had checked in to receive in-patient care. "I'm getting back to being my old self," Marvin said. "You were right. I needed this. When they release me, I'm going to drive down to my mother's house and enter the Day Treatment Program at Roger Williams Medical Center. Just wanted to let you know that I've got things under control."

EPILOGUE

The torturous 20-month wait was about to end. Barnes was finally going to receive the opportunity to defend himself against a felony charge of solicitation of a child, a seventeen-year-old girl.

Four days prior to his scheduled appearance in Rhode Island Superior Court, he called me from Providence. It was the first time we had spoken in three months.

"Hey, Mikey, I'm going to war. Got to be in court at 9 a.m. on Monday. You coming down?" he asked. "I need you in my corner, man."

"I'll be there," I told him, "but tell me how you're doing."

"Staying strong," he said, reciting his favorite catchphrase. "I had a couple little slips, but once I win this case, I'm going down to Virginia and get treatment in the Victory in Jesus program. God's honest truth."

His slurred words and jittery speech pattern left no doubt in my mind that he was high at that very moment.

"Marvin, do yourself a favor and lay off the drugs," I said. You've got to be totally straight when you walk into court."

"Just wanted to check in. Love ya, brother," he said before abruptly hanging up.

Entering the brick-faced courthouse on September 8, 2014, I headed to the Clerk's Office where an employee looked up Barnes's case number on his computer and directed me to Part Four of the Criminal Division.

From the doorway of Judge Jeffrey Lanphear's courtroom, I scanned the rows of spectator benches, hoping to spot Marvin. There was no sign of him.

I asked a court officer if the case might have been postponed. He flipped through his copy of the judge's docket and said, "I don't see Marvin Barnes's name at all. Even if the trial got pushed back, it would be listed in these papers. It's strange that the Clerk's Office told you it was scheduled for today."

Outside the courthouse, I phoned Barnes. My call went straight to voicemail. There was nothing I could do but head back to Boston.

Five minutes into the drive up Interstate 95, my cell phone rang. The call was from Barnes's ex-wife, Debbe. "Mike, Marvin passed away early this morning," she said, sobbing while barely being able to get the words out. "Some guy he was staying with in Providence found him lying in bed and couldn't wake him up. By the time the EMTs arrived, there was nothing that could be done."

I expressed my sympathy to her but didn't bother to ask what the cause of death was. I already knew. Directly or indirectly, cocaine had claimed another victim. (Two months later, the Rhode Island Medical Examiner's Office ruled that Barnes had died from "acute cocaine and heroin intoxication.")

Can't say I was shocked by the news of his passing. Just the opposite, I saw this coming months ago. My hunch was that Marvin did too.

My mind raced back to the final month of his stay at my home. I remembered, almost word for word, one particular heated exchange between us that took place on the day I had discovered he had gone back to using coke. As we yelled back and forth, I called him a "useless junkie" simply to get a rise out of him.

"Stop calling me names," he shouted back. "What you just don't get is that I have a disease."

"Yeah, but it's a *treatable* disease," I said. "Quit making excuses, stop feeling sorry for yourself, and go get some professional help before all the cocaine that you're putting into your system kills you."

Sadly, my words of warning had suddenly turned into a haunting prophecy.

When I arrived home, I phoned Bob Costas. He had already heard the news. "Unfortunately, Marvin's epitaph is going to read: 'Squandered Talent,'" he said. "It's always been my belief that had he lived up to his potential, he would have made it into the Hall of Fame. That's how much natural ability he had.

"Wherever Marvin played, he created one problem after another. Still, his charisma, charm, and tremendous sense of humor made him such an affable person that coaches and team-mates, with a few exceptions, were always willing to overlook his character flaws."

As I opened the door to the bedroom where Marvin had stayed, my eyes were drawn to the lone memento remaining on his bureau: a large gold-framed picture of him smiling, sur-rounded by a group of ten teenagers who were in the Men to Men program. The black and white photo spoke volumes about how proud he had been to have made such a meaningful impact on so many young people's lives.

Now those noble efforts had ended in tragic irony: The ultimate lesson he taught his students about the dangers of drugs had come through his own death.

I recalled the many times he had discussed his efforts to defeat what he perceived as insidious evil spirits that sought to shred his willpower. "It's like I can hear them calling out my name, trying to sucker me into their trap and destroy me, body and soul," Marvin once said. "With my addiction, I can never say 'I won the war.' I just have to be a soldier, ready to stand up and fight a new battle every day until they give up and disappear."

But in his case, whether he realized it or not, those insidious demons never vanished. Instead, they lurked in the back of his mind, waiting patiently for the perfect moment to strike. It took forty years, but they had accomplished their mission.

In the early morning hours of September 8, 2014, Marvin Barnes finally hit rock bottom. There would be no miraculous, uplifting ending to his life story. For him, "The Race" had ended all too soon.

Have They Gone?; retired *Boston Herald* and *Baltimore Sun* news editor Tom Gibbons; Mark Purdy of the *San Jose Mercury News*; *Houston Chronicle* columnist Michael Murphy; Dave Whitehorn of *Newsday*; and Shira Springer and Bob Ryan of the *Boston Globe*.

Thanks also to Rick and Donna Carlisle, Bill Walton, Julius Erving, Derek Sanderson, Ernie DiGregorio, Kevin Stacom, Mark McAndrew, Fran Costello, the late Dave Gavitt, the late Dr. Jack Ramsay, the late John Bach, Doug Collins, Ed Ratleff, Tommy Heinsohn, Tom Henderson, Charles Grantham, Wally Rooney, John Lucas, the late Ozzie Silna, the late Harry Weltman, Gus Gerard, Steve "Snapper" Jones, Ron Boone, Mike D'Antoni, Don Chaney, Mike Barr, Barry Parkhill, M. L. Carr, Freddie Lewis, the late Maurice Lucas, Dave Cowens, Larry Brown, Herb Brown, Doug Moe, Tom "Satch" Sanders, Gene Shue, Oscar Feldman, Bob MacKinnon Jr., Dave Lewin, Hubie Brown, Jan Volk, Rick Weitzman, John Y. Brown, Roosevelt Becton, Providence SID Arthur Parks, John Treacy, Jane Ford, and the late Jimmy Adams.

Also critical to the book's accuracy was the cooperation of law enforcement officials Damian Farley Sr., Mike Reap, Richard Byrne, Chuck Visco, Patrick Lynch, Det. Richard Vogel, Brendan Doherty, Gregg Schwarz, Herman Groman, and the late Dan McCarthy.

The author would like to acknowledge the assistance of Derek and Renate Vogel, Preston and Joan Carlisle, Attorney Bill Carlisle, Jack Fox, Attorney Ryan Lewis, Ashley and Jill Wipfler, John Dennis, Don Worden, Sean Downey, Ron Kolodziej, George Hailer, Glenn Frank, Erik Hailer, Valerie Pawson, Casey Gibbons, Phil Wall, Tom Norton, Evan Kulak, Michael Russell, Joseph Ingegneri, Ginny Alverson, Damian Farley Jr., Brett Tyson, Dan and Paul Graham, Paul Nichols, Mike Wile, Keith Levitre, Pauline Downing, Jim Katz, Kenny Katz, Greg McGinty, Michael and Brendan McGinty, Chris Ensminger, Greg Lynch, Bill DeMedio, Leslie Droogan, Suzanne Rosenwasser, Andy Curtis, Dr. Arnold Scheller, and Gail Weisberg.